PARADISE CANCELLED

PARADISE CANCELLED

UNVEILING THE FALSE PROMISES OF A SECULARIST UTOPIA

Anthony Schratz

True Freedom Press

Disclaimer Notice

Table of Contents

Acknowledgements

This book has been some years in the making, and many people have contributed to it to a greater or lesser degree. I would here like to acknowledge some of those whose contributions have been most helpful.

I am grateful to my friends Jacek Bacz, Richard Bastien, Patrick Duffley, Paul Tomory, Riley McGuire, and David Wang, each of whom took the trouble to read my entire manuscript and provide valuable suggestions that I incorporated into the final version.

I would like to thank my friend, Jason Gennaro, for his help with the introduction. And special thanks to my brother, Joe Schratz, and my niece, Michelle Wyse, for their insightful comments on Chapter 2. Many thanks as well to my friend, Qizhou Cui, who provided valuable input on Chapters 3 and 4 and to Gabriel Freitas for his comments on Chapter 5.

Special thanks also to my friend, Angelo Roldan, for his input regarding the cover design and to whom I owe the title of the book, and to Scott Ventureyra for his work in editing, formatting, and publishing the book.

Finally, I am grateful to all the residents of Ernescliff College to whom I presented the ideas contained in this book in a series of talks and who challenged me each time with perceptive questions.

In honour of St. Josemaria Escriva,
whose teachings have shaped my life.

You have made us for Yourself, Lord, and our hearts
are restless until they find their rest in Thee.

(Augustine, Confessions, 1.1.1)

Introduction

For many years, I have been the director of university centers that aim to prepare young men for the challenges awaiting them in life by helping them become virtuous leaders. We seek to promote academic excellence, high personal standards, dedication to family and friends, openness to those in need, and a spirit of service to the community. We try to help them unlock their enormous potential and inspire them to give of themselves. It has always been a rewarding experience, one that fills me with great joy. One of its appealing aspects is to see how idealistic and driven these young men are. They tend to value peace and seek to practice empathy, service, and compassion; to be kind and generous; and to help those in need. They have a concern for the environment, and they sincerely want to work towards the elimination of disease, ignorance, and poverty in order to make the world a better place. The noble values of freedom, justice, equality, tolerance, and human rights particularly captivate them.

These young men naturally gravitate toward the current worldview that permeates our society as they strive to live out these values. This new worldview does not have an official name. In accordance with our analysis of it in Chapter 2, in this book we refer to it mainly as Expressive Individualism, but also from time to time as Secular Individualism, the Autonomous Individual, the Modern Self, etc.

This worldview promises a paradise characterized by these values of freedom, justice, equality, tolerance, and human rights. The ideal of redressing historical injustices experienced by minorities draws these young men, and they harbor a strong desire to assist those less fortunate. They have a firm belief in autonomy and moral relativism within the limits set by the Do No Harm principle: my freedom must not impinge on the freedom of others. They also embrace the Golden Rule: always treat others the way you would like them to treat you.

At the same time, there is a feeling among many of these young men that there is trouble in paradise. They detect serious cracks in the secularist façade and sense that there is something missing in the promise of this utopia. Their own experience tells them that the paradise promised by autonomous individualism is illusory and is missing some of the key components needed to make them happy and fulfilled, as well as to make the world the better place they wish it to be. They tend to admire Jordan Peterson and others like him, whose podcasts and videos provide them with a freshness of vision and more self-confidence. Listening to these speakers equips them with the necessary elements to challenge the ideals of Expressive Individualism, yet they lack the intellectual formation required to craft a rigorous critique of this ideology. They do not know what a viable alternative might look like, and they do not believe that Christianity and the natural law, properly understood, are what they are looking for.

So, this book is aimed firstly at those who are looking for a simple, clear, substantial, and easy-to-read explanation of both the Christian worldview and that of Expressive Individualism, and the contradictions inherent in the latter. It will be useful for Christians who know and practice their faith but who want to be able to articulate a serious critique of Expressive Individualism. Christians whose faith has been lost or shaken due to this worldview will also find it useful. It can help them understand that Expressive Individualism's assault on Christianity is entirely without intellectual merit.

Those who have no religion and who hold the worldview of Expressive Individualism simply because it has become the default position in our society should find something for themselves, too. Many people have unintentionally absorbed this position from society. They have been told that religion is basically superstition, and that Christians are intolerant, dogmatic, narrow-minded, and judgmental people who engage in hate speech. Therefore, they lack the motivation to delve deeper into Christianity. This book will hopefully move them to give some serious consideration to what the Christian tradition teaches.

The structure of this book is as follows:

Chapter 1 sets out the Christian worldview.

Chapter 2 makes the case for Expressive Individualism.

Chapter 3 compares and contrasts the two worldviews, demonstrating how Expressive Individualism displaced Christianity as the dominant worldview in the West.

Chapter 4 makes the case for Natural Law, the existence of which Expressive Individualism denies.

Chapter 5 aims to demonstrate that Christianity is truly responsible for the great achievements claimed by the Modern Self.

Chapter 6 exposes an ostensible contradiction in the worldview of Expressive Individualism and shows how it deals with it.

Chapter 7 analyzes several inconsistencies inherent in Expressive Individualism.

Chapter 8 provides a game plan for the Christian, showing how he can still thrive and spread his faith in a society that embraces Expressive Individualism and how this, in the end, will make him happy and fulfilled.

It is my hope that this book will prove useful to those seeking to make sense of our current situation.

Chapter 1

The Christian Worldview

The Christian worldview generally held sway in Western Europe and the Americas up until the 18th century. Since then, it has slowly given way to a new worldview that emphasizes personal autonomy and individualism.

We will look at the Christian worldview in general and then focus more particularly on those areas where it clashes with Expressive Individualism: its understanding of the human person, of the meaning and purpose of life, love, marriage, family, sexuality and sexual identity, and the nature and purpose of the state and society.

Catholicism, Protestantism, and Eastern Orthodoxy articulate certain aspects of the Christian worldview somewhat differently. Here we will outline the Catholic version of the Christian worldview, which has a single, clearly defined doctrine and is the one that has most shaped Western Civilization.

The Nature of God, the Creation of the World, and the Nature of Man

The Catholic worldview holds that an eternal, infinitely good, infinitely powerful, transcendent God created the universe with perfect freedom. This is the one and only God. He is pure spirit, perfect in every way, self-subsistent, and completely independent from His creation. He has no needs, is infinitely happy, and subsists in absolute and everlasting joy.

Although there is only one God, He exists in a Trinity of persons: Father, Son, and Holy Spirit. There is only one divine nature, but there are three divine persons. This Trinity of persons is an eternal communion of self-giving love, as Pope John Paul II states: "God in his deepest mystery is not a solitude, but a family, since he has in himself fatherhood, sonship and the essence of the family, which is love."[1] Thus, God can never be lonely.

---

1   John Paul II, *Homily of His Holiness, John Paul II, Puebla de Los Angeles (Mexico), Palafox Major Seminary*, Vatican website, January 28, 1979, https://www.vatican.va/content/john-paul-ii/en/homilies/1979/documents/hf_jp-ii_hom_19790128_messico-puebla-seminario.html.

As the Catechism of the Catholic Church also emphasizes,

> The mystery of the Most Holy Trinity is the central mystery of Christian faith and life. It is the mystery of God in himself. It is therefore the source of all the other mysteries of faith… It is the most fundamental and essential teaching in the "hierarchy of the truths of faith." The whole history of salvation is identical with the history of the way and the means by which the one true God, Father, Son and Holy Spirit, reveals himself to men "and reconciles and unites with himself those who turn away from sin."[2]

God created the universe and man to show forth and share his goodness with mankind in an act of absolute and infinite love. This essentially means that God loved man into existence. So mankind and the universe exist only because of an act of God's will. He gave man existence in an act of infinite love. All of creation reflects his goodness and wisdom.

Furthermore, God created man in His image and likeness, meaning that man resembles God in certain ways.[3] And God gave man a calling to possess eternal happiness in Heaven with him after leading a life of love and holiness on earth. Therefore, God destined man to spend eternity in heaven in a union so utterly intimate that we can't even begin to imagine the happiness it will entail.

Of all God's creatures in the material universe, only man has a rational intellect and free will. Only man is able to know and love his creator: "He alone is called to share, by knowledge and love, in God's own life. It was for this end that he was created, and this is the fundamental reason for his dignity."[4] So, through God's grace, man can enter into an intimate and loving union with God that transcends his natural abilities and elevates him to a divine level of existence. By accepting God's grace through faith, a man is divinized in the sense that, through the indwelling of the Holy Spirit, he is able to participate in God's own life and thereby experience a profound union with God, growing in holiness and virtue. Man is a being that is both corporeal and spiritual, with a material body as well as a spiritual and immortal soul. However, in man, spirit and matter are not two separate natures united; rather, their union forms a single human nature.

Adam and Eve in Paradise

The first book of the Bible (the Book of Genesis) sets out the story of the creation of man and his subsequent fall from grace in symbolic terms.[5]

---

2   Catechism of the Catholic Church, 2nd ed. (Vatican City: Vatican Press, 1997), 234.
3   Catechism of the Catholic Church, 355.
4   Catechism of the Catholic Church, 356.
5   Catechism of the Catholic Church, 375.

It demonstrates how God created Adam and Eve, our first ancestors, in a state of goodness, friendship, and harmony within themselves, with each other, and with all of creation.

God placed our first parents in the Garden of Eden and endowed them with great gifts over and above their human nature. These included, for example, freedom from suffering and death and control of their passions by reason. But it also included sanctifying grace, which is a participation in the divine nature, the life of God Himself in the soul. Through this grace, Adam and Eve's human nature was elevated so that they were able to commune with God as a preparation for their eternal life with him in heaven.

Even though God created man in his image and established him in his friendship, our first parents were still subject to the laws of creation and to the moral norms that governed the use of their freedom. This is symbolized in Genesis as the prohibition against *eating of the fruit of the tree of the knowledge of good and evil.* These moral norms were not at all arbitrary. They rather flowed from man's nature and from his last end. Adam and Eve would have known these norms intuitively.[6]

Eating of the fruit of the tree of the knowledge of good and evil meant not only knowing good and evil but wanting to have a say in what is good and evil, what is forbidden and allowed, to be independent of God. It is the sin of all ages. It is man's constant temptation to decide what is right and wrong, good and evil, by his own judgement and caprice, and not to regulate his conduct according to the law of God, which is in accordance with his nature. It is a refusal by man to accept his status as a creature, a being created by God and subject to his creator. It would mean choosing to rebel against God's law of self-giving built into man's nature and opting for self-assertion and autonomy.

The Fall of Man and its Consequences

As we read in the Third Chapter of Genesis, Adam and Eve ate of the fruit of the tree of the knowledge of good and evil. They sinned by rejecting God's law and seeking to be a law unto themselves. Human happiness depends on acting in accord with our nature, which entails self-giving. Adam and Eve rejected self-giving and opted for autonomy and self-assertion. This original sin, as it is called, would have dire consequences for the happiness of mankind.

In fact, the consequences of their sin were immediate. The harmony in which Adam and Eve had found themselves was destroyed. The control of the passions by man's reason was shattered; the union of man and woman became subject to tensions, their relations henceforth marked by lust and dominance.

6   Catechism of the Catholic Church, 396.

Harmony with creation was broken, and visible creation became alien and hostile to man. And the gift of immortality was also lost: death makes its entrance into human history.[7]

The most serious consequence of original sin, however, was the loss of that bond of intimate union with God, which we call sanctifying grace. The Fall put an end to the friendship between God and man. From that moment on, heaven was closed to mankind, and man was in a state of enmity with God, condemned to eternal damnation unless pardoned by God.

For original sin was not Adam's sin alone. By God's decree, he was the representative of the entire human race. He sinned, and all mankind must suffer the consequences. Because our human nature fell from grace in its very origin, we inherit from Adam a human nature that is fallen. We say that we are born in the state of original sin.

What is this original sin that we are all born with? It is essentially a privation: something that is absent from the soul, something that ought to be there—the supernatural life, which we call sanctifying grace. This means that we are born with a soul that is spiritually dead insofar as supernatural life is concerned.

The consequences of original sin to Adam's descendants are manifestly obvious in our own experience. For we all suffer from concupiscence, that propensity to sin that plagues us all. We find ourselves drawn towards what is wrong and sunk in many evils. Our inclination towards evil cannot be understood apart from the fact that Adam has transmitted this original sin to us.

Original sin constituted an offence of great magnitude against God. This is difficult for us to understand. We tend to look upon sin as something almost inevitable, given the fact that we are weak, ignorant, and frequently tempted. Our passions constantly urge us to engage in sinful behaviour. However, before the Fall, Adam and Eve were not weak or ignorant, and they had complete control over their passions. They deliberately chose autonomy from God, rejection of God, without any extenuating circumstances. This rendered their sin far more serious than any sin that we might commit. Since God is infinitely good and had endowed Adam and Eve with an overabundance of gifts, their sin really constituted a terrible offence against God.

After original sin, on his own, man could not re-establish friendship with God. This friendship implies forgiveness of sin, and only God, as the One who had been offended, could extend that forgiveness. In addition, it implies re-acquisition of grace, which is something supernatural, above man's nature. So, no merely natural effort on man's part could attain this. Being spiritually dead as a result of original sin, man could not perform an act of supernatural value and so could not restore this friendship, in the same way that a dead man cannot bring himself back to life.[8]

---

7   Catechism of the Catholic Church, 400.

8   Cf. Fernando Ocariz, L.F. Mateo Seco and J.A. Riestra, *The Mystery of Jesus Christ* (Portland, Oregon: Four Courts Press, 1994), 32-33.

The Redemption

After his fall, man was not abandoned by God. On the contrary, God promised to send a Saviour or Redeemer into the world to save man from his sins, to restore man's friendship with God and to open the gates of heaven to mankind once again.

God began this process by creating for Himself a people (the Jewish race, the Chosen People) and revealing Himself to them, starting with Abraham, over a period of almost two thousand years. His revelation to this people through the Mosaic Law and the prophets would prepare mankind for the coming of the Redeemer, who would be born from among this people.

God could have redeemed mankind in other ways. He could simply have forgiven us. However, the way he did it was most in keeping with divine justice. He chose the most sublime way. Since the original sin had been committed by a man, it was most fitting that a man should make up for that sin. But since an act of supernatural value was required to effect perfect reparation, that act would have to be performed by God. So, the most fitting way to achieve the Redemption was for a man who was also God to carry out an act of supernatural value. Hence the Second Person of the Blessed Trinity, also known as the Word of God, would take on human nature in the person of Jesus Christ, and thus representing all humanity, would redeem us through his passion and death on the cross.

Jesus Christ is the fullness of God's Revelation. He is the second person of the Blessed Trinity whom the Father sent into the world to become man in order to save the world from sin. He is the fullness of revelation because, up until the time of Christ, God spoke to men and revealed Himself to them through prophets. In Christ, God Himself took on human nature in the womb of the Virgin Mary and lived among us as a man. Jesus Christ is the center of human history. The Lord of History. All human history from the Fall leads up to the coming of Christ, and all history after Christ flows away from it.

So the Word became flesh for us in the person of Jesus Christ, in order to save us by reconciling us with God, who loved us and sent his Son to be the expiation for our sins. In addition, the Word became flesh so that we might know God's love: "For God so loved the world that he gave his only begotten Son, that whoever believes in him should not perish but have eternal life."[9]

Another reason for the Incarnation was so that in Christ we would have a model of holiness. We are called to pray to the One God, who is pure spirit. Such a God can seem distant, and establishing a loving relationship with him can appear difficult. But this task has been rendered far easier since the Incarnation,

---

9   Jn. 3:16 (Revised Standard Version, Second Catholic Edition).

since we can now also pray to God by praying to Jesus and identifying ourselves with him, for he is a man like us. "By His incarnation the Son of God has united Himself in some fashion with every man. He worked with human hands, He thought with a human mind, acted by human choice and loved with a human heart. Born of the Virgin Mary, He has truly been made one of us, like us in all things except sin."[10] His most holy humanity is the bridge that leads us to our Father God. He is the model for the Beatitudes and the norm of the new law: "Love one another as I have loved you."[11] This love implies an effective offering of oneself, after his example. Finally, the Son of God became man so that man, by entering into communion with the Word, might become a son of God, as we will see below.

The Holy Spirit conceived Jesus in the virginal womb of Mary miraculously, without the intervention of any man. Jesus was born and lived at the beginning of the First Century A.D. in Nazareth, a village in Palestine, engaged in his father's trade. When he was around thirty years old, he began preaching and performing miracles. This drew down on Him the jealousy and ire of the local elites, who denounced Him to the Roman governor as an insurrectionist. He was condemned to death and crucified.

Just as man had sinned by refusing to give God His love (a refusal expressed in the act of disobedience, which is sin), so Christ's work of redemption was in the form of an act of infinitely perfect love, expressed in an act of infinitely perfect obedience to His Father God, that comprised his whole life upon earth.

Since he was God, any single act of His done with the intention of redeeming us from our sins would have been an act of infinite value and so would have sufficed to effect our redemption. Why, then, did Christ decide to undergo his passion? Why did He give himself up to be humiliated, scourged, crowned with thorns, and crucified? He did so to show us the horror of sin, to illustrate His immense love for us, and to demonstrate the great value that we have in God's eyes.

Jesus died to free us from our sins and redeem us from the slavery that sin had introduced into mankind's life. By offering his life to God on the cross, Jesus instituted the New Covenant, that is to say, the new form of union of God with men. The sacrifice of the Cross purified mankind from sin. It was a sacrifice of atonement and reparation for sin. It restored man's friendship with God and opened up the way of salvation for mankind.

On the third day after dying on the cross, Christ rose from the dead and, after forty days, ascended into heaven after giving His Apostles the mission to spread the Gospel.

---

10 Second Vatican Council, "Pastoral Constitution on the Church in the Modern World, Gaudium et Spes, December 7, 1965", https://www.vatican.va/archive/hist_councils/ii_vatican_council/documents/vat-ii_cons_19651207_gaudium-et-spes_en.html, sec. 22 (hereafter cited as GS).

11 Jn. 15:12 (Revised Standard Version, Second Catholic Edition).

The Church

Before ascending into heaven, Christ founded his Church. The Church is a complex reality, and no single definition can do it justice. The aspect of the Church that is important for us here is that it is the institution that continues the work of redemption with the aid of the Holy Spirit by applying the merits that Christ won on the Cross to individuals throughout the course of history.

Its mission is the salvation of souls. It is a continuation of the redemptive work of Christ on Earth, which it carries out through the offering of the Sacrifice of the Mass, through the sacraments, its preaching, its teaching, and its law and discipline. The Church has no temporal or worldly aim. It is not a political party, nor a social ideology, nor a worldwide organization for harmony or material progress, even though these are noble in their own right. The Church proclaims to all that our destiny is eternal and supernatural, that only in Christ are we saved, and that only in Him will we achieve in some way true peace and happiness in this life. So, the Church has an exclusively supernatural aim and mission.

The Meaning and Purpose of Life

From all that we have seen up until now, it is clear that the Church has a precise teaching on the nature of man and the world and on the meaning of life. The Church teaches that the universe has a purpose, which is to reflect the glory of God and to serve man in his quest for holiness.

Man also has a purpose. That purpose is to lead a virtuous life of self-giving love in an intimate union with God in Christ through the Church on earth, and then to be eternally happy with God in heaven. This is the purpose of man's existence. A man is free to decide how he is going to lead his life, but the purpose of his life is given to him. By his choices, he either achieves this purpose or not.

So, the Christian is called to lead a life of love and self-giving to others. The New Commandment that Christ gave Christians was: "Love one another as I have loved you." And how did Christ love us? By dying on the Cross. And for whom did Christ die? For everyone and for each one individually, even those who were torturing Him to death. So, the Christian is called to love everyone without exception, and to consider no one His enemy. He is to spend his life loving others, which means wanting what is good for them and, making the effort to bring about that good. A Christian's life should be a great adventure of love, a great love affair.

One becomes a Christian through Baptism, which fills the soul with sanctifying grace, thereby elevating the soul itself and enabling it to live in communion with God, to act by his love, to live and act in keeping with God's call to holiness. "God's love has been poured into our hearts through the Holy Spirit."[12]

Of course, Baptism does not work like some magic potion. In order to receive Baptism validly with all its effects, one must have faith, which is an adherence of the whole person to God. Through faith we believe all that God reveals, we trust that he will fulfill his promises, and we obey what he commands.

The first influx of sanctifying grace that is received in Baptism effects a real change in a man. It configures his soul to Christ, making him an adopted child of God and hence a member of God's household and a coheir of Heaven with Christ. So the Christian is someone made in the image and likeness of God, redeemed by the precious blood of Christ, made a son of God by Baptism, called to pursue a life of holiness on earth and to eternal happiness with God in heaven. That is his identity. That is who he is.

As an "adopted son," the Christian can truly call God "Father" in union with the Son. When someone is adopted into a family, he does not share that family's blood line. But the adoption effected by sanctifying grace identifies a man with Christ to such an extent that he becomes a "partaker of the divine nature."[13] Yes, this grace is a participation in the life of God Himself. It introduces man into the intimacy of Trinitarian life. It is the divine life in his soul, so he becomes a temple of God, who dwells in his soul in grace.[14]

Christ is "the firstborn among many brethren."[15] He is the firstborn to the life of grace. And all Christians are called to put off the old man of concupiscence and to "put on Christ"[16]: to imitate Him, to follow Him, to identify themselves with Him, to be transformed in Christ so that they can truly say, "It is no longer I who live but Christ who lives in me."[17] Now this task of transformation in Christ is something supernatural (i.e., above our nature and so beyond our natural ability to attain)—it is the work of grace. And it is the Holy Spirit who effects this transformation, who continuously moulds the image of Christ in us. However, that work of our sanctification requires our cooperation, which mainly consists in removing obstacles to the sanctifying action of the Holy Spirit by a constant struggle against pride, sensuality, laziness, etc.

God endowed man with free will. And this freedom also has a purpose: it allows man to choose the good, to pursue his end, and to love God freely. God also endowed man with a rational intellect. This intellect allows man to know the truth. For without knowing the truth about who he is and why he was created, man cannot pursue his end.

---

12   Rom. 5:5 (Revised Standard Version, Second Catholic Edition).
13   2 Pet. 1:4 (Revised Standard Version, Second Catholic Edition).
14   Catechism of the Catholic Church, 1997.
15   Rom. 8:29 (Revised Standard Version, Second Catholic Edition).
16   Gal. 3:27 (Revised Standard Version, Second Catholic Edition).
17   Gal. 2:20 (Revised Standard Version, Second Catholic Edition).

The Natural Law, Freedom and Truth

The Christian Tradition teaches that the natural moral law (also called the natural law or the moral law) is written on the heart of each man. It consists of those principles that indicate how we should lead our lives if we want to thrive and be happy in this life and the next: to fulfill our great potential, achieve the end for which we were created, and become the kind of person we were meant to be, which is the only way for us to be truly happy.

The natural moral law is like the instruction manual of a machine. The machine does not function according to the manual because of what is written in the instruction manual. Rather, the instruction manual is simply stating how the machine functions because that is how it is made. In the same way, something is not morally right or wrong because the natural law so states it. On the contrary, the natural moral law simply sets out what is good or evil (good or bad for us) because of our human nature—the way we are made and because of our last end. So, it is not a law superimposed on life from outside, making it more difficult. It simply sets out the conditions that make authentic freedom and fruitful love possible.

The natural law is written on the heart of every man. As we will see in Chapter 4, this means that the most basic principles of the natural law are known and are indeed self-evident to reason, so that when a person reaches the age of reason, he becomes aware of these basic principles. As J. Budziszewski has stated, they are "things we can't not know."[18] They include the basic principle of morality, which is to do good and avoid evil. But they also comprise other basic moral norms: don't harm others, don't steal what rightfully belongs to someone else, do not take an innocent human life, etc.

We are tempted to choose goods that will give us immediate gratification or pleasure over others that are better for us. When we choose independence from God by violating the moral law, we abuse our freedom and do damage to ourselves. We also become less free because we become slaves to our passions and appetites. We diminish our ability to choose the good. Drugs and alcohol are extreme examples of this, but every sin negatively affects our freedom.

Following the moral law gives us this freedom, a freedom not shared by those who do not follow it. It is true self-mastery, the capacity to choose the things that make for our happiness and for the common good, to lead a full life, to develop our God-given capacity to grow in virtue. We are called to greatness, and the moral law is the roadmap that leads us there. False freedom, i.e., total personal autonomy, doing what we feel like doing, and simply following our instincts, undermines our true humanity in that it prevents us from flourishing

---

18 J. Budziszewski, *What We Can't Not Know* (Dallas: Spence Publishing Company, 2003), Chapter 2.

as human beings. It leads to addictions and attachments and makes us slaves to our disordered tendencies and base passions.

Because it is based on our human nature and on our purpose, which do not change, the natural moral law is absolute, objective, and universal. It cannot be relative or subjective. It can't depend on our good intentions or our feelings. If it did, then we would be unable to condemn as immoral heinous crimes committed by people who believe that their actions are somehow good (e.g.; terrorists, suicide bombers, those who engage in genocide, etc.). It is true that, morally, an action can be objectively wrong in that it infringes the natural law, but the culpability of the person carrying out the action might be diminished because of ignorance or other reasons. This is a complex question that is dealt with in depth by Catholic moral teaching.[19]

Of course, Christian Moral Teaching goes well beyond the Natural Law, which can only provide man with the basic principles of morality. Through Jesus Christ, God has revealed a far deeper and richer moral law. It is only by following this Biblical Morality, this law of love, with the help of grace, that a man can undergo that transformation in Christ mentioned above. A Christian who truly seeks to be transformed in Christ will lead a virtuous life of self-sacrificing love and engage in a lifelong struggle against his pride, sensuality, laziness, selfishness, etc. Following the Beatitudes, he will become more and more identified with Jesus Christ, seeking to live all the virtues to a heroic degree.

The Christian worldview stresses that we are created by God for a purpose, and that fact bestows purpose on everything. Our human nature is given to us. We do not decide on what it is. The purpose of our life is also given to us. We decide the means we want to use to attain that goal, and we can even make the grave mistake of choosing another goal, but the goal itself has been determined for us by God, and the pursuit of any other goal will not lead to human flourishing and happiness. Christianity teaches that immediately after death, each man will be judged by God on how he has lived the moral law and will be rewarded or punished accordingly and forever. God condemns no one to Hell. Those who end up in Hell have made that decision themselves by the choices they deliberately made while on earth. The Particular Judgment is God's acknowledgement of the choice we made to either accept His love or reject it. One's actions on earth have eternal consequences.

---

19   Dr Ralph Martin, STD, *Considering Culpability*, Homiletic and Pastoral Review, June 28, 2017, https://www.hprweb.com/2017/06/considering-culpability/.

Marriage, Family, Sexuality and Human Life

Christianity also has a teaching with respect to marriage, the family, sexuality, the human person, and human life. This teaching flows necessarily from all that we have seen so far. In the Book of Genesis, we read: "Then the Lord God said, 'It is not good that the man should be alone.'" The human person has a radical need to enter into relationships with others. We are relational beings, social animals. We have a need not only to interact with others but to establish a deeper relationship with some people. We naturally seek some close companions, people with whom we can share our lives and give ourselves to. Man is the only one of God's creatures who needs, desires, and is capable of loving and giving himself to another. And he does so in the hope that the other will do the same to him, that the love and self-giving will be mutual. This is essentially the basis of human friendship.

Among these relationships, there is one that is special. Each person desires a soulmate, someone with whom he will enter into a loving, complete, and more intimate relationship, someone with whom he will share his whole life. It will go beyond other friendships in that it will also include an element of erotic love and intimacy and will entail a deeper gift of self. This relationship will help give meaning and purpose to his life, and in it he will find fulfillment. So he will seek to make this relationship as perfect and complete as possible.

In order for this relationship to work, the two lovers must complement each other. And since we are sexualized beings, this complementarity can only take place if the loved one is someone of the other sex. It is also obvious that if this self-giving to one's loved one is to be total and complete, it must be exclusive. One can't make a complete gift of oneself to more than one person. And finally, a complete self-giving must be permanent. One can't give oneself to another completely today while reserving the right to abandon the person tomorrow. Thus, according to the Christian Tradition, man has been created as a sexual being so that he can make a gift of himself to a person of the opposite sex, and that this gift by its very nature must be complete, mutual, exclusive, and permanent. Our sexuality makes possible the physical expression of that gift in a profound way. As Edward Sri has said:

> Since God exists as a communion of three divine Persons giving themselves completely in love to each other, man and woman—created in the image of the Trinity—are not made to live as isolated individuals, each seeking their own pleasure and advantage from the other. Rather, man and woman are made to live in an intimate personal communion of self-giving love, mirroring the inner life of the Trinity.[20]

20 Edward Sri, *Men, Women and the Mystery of Love* (Cincinnati, Ohio: Franciscan Media, 2015), 152.

Love and Life

The Book of Genesis also tells us that after God had created them male and female, he told them: "Increase and multiply, and fill the earth, and subdue it."[21] So the command to generate new human life came about as a result of Adam and Eve being made male and female. God created an intrinsic link between the procreative faculty and the consummation of sexual love. New human persons were to be conceived and born as a result of the mutual gift of self between a man and a woman as expressed in the sexual act.

Why has God established that link between our sexuality and the bringing of new life into the world. Why has he united life and love? A careful reading of Genesis shows us that this was part of the original plan: "And God created man in his own image; in the image of God he created him; male and female he created them."[22] So somehow, being created male and female is a consequence of being created in the image of God. How can we understand this? We can start by reminding ourselves that the one God is Three Divine Persons who love each other infinitely and who lovingly give themselves to each other in a way that is mutual and eternal. We should also recall that God's love is fruitful, leading to life. We have been created as a result of God's love. He essentially loved us into existence. Since we are created in God's image, he wanted a husband's and wife's mutual love to be fruitful as well, to bring about new life. In a sense, we can say that, through God's design, the spouses are allowed to participate in God's creative power. He wanted each new human being to be the fruit of an act of love. Therefore, the Church teaches that each human person is called to make a complete, mutual, exclusive, and permanent gift of himself to a person of the opposite sex. Since it is our sexuality that makes the physical expression of that self-giving possible, the sexual act must only take place in the context of the permanent commitment that we call marriage. Furthermore, that permanent relationship must maintain the unity between love and life and so be open to God's creative power. If self-giving is to be complete, it must include one's fertility—the capacity to bring new life into the world.

Marriage and the Family

Undoubtedly, marriage also has a purpose. In marriage, God calls a man and a woman to an intimate and indissoluble communion of life and love. It is ordered to the communion and good of the couple and to the procreation and education of children.[23] Parents (and not the State) have the primary

---

21   Gen. 1:28 (Douay-Rheims 1899 American Edition).
22   Gen. 1:27 (Douay-Rheims 1899 American Edition).
23   Catechism of the Catholic Church, 1601.

responsibility for the education and upbringing of their children. The parents begin the process of giving life, and they are called to bring it to fruition in the context of their marriage. And since the marriage bond is by its very nature permanent and hence indissoluble, divorce is morally unacceptable. And the family also has a purpose. In creating man and woman, God instituted the human family and endowed it with its fundamental constitution: one man and one woman united in marriage, together with their children. The family is a communion of persons, a sign and image of the communion of the Trinity: God the Father and the Son in the Holy Spirit.

Furthermore, "the family is the original cell of social life. It is the natural society in which husband and wife are called to give themselves in love and in the gift of life. Authority, stability, and a life of relationships within the family constitute the foundations for freedom, security, and fraternity within society...Family life is an initiation into life in society."[24] In the family, children are socialized and learn the virtues necessary for life in society: love, respect, courtesy, service, honesty, understanding, forgiveness, order, responsibility, sincerity, work, etc. Because of this, society has the grave duty to support and strengthen marriage and the family, to recognize their true nature, to foster and protect them, and to safeguard public morality.

The Virtue of Chastity

Given the above understanding of human sexuality, we can understand the virtue of chastity, or what it means to lead a pure life: someone is pure when he or she makes use of his/her sexuality only as the physical expression of a mutual, complete, exclusive, and permanent gift of self to another person. When exercised in this context, our sexuality brings incredible fulfillment, leads to great happiness, and becomes a source of union. Furthermore, it's a path of holiness: the marital bed is an altar in which a pleasing sacrifice is offered to God. Impure behavior, on the other hand, can be described as any use of sexuality opposed to chastity. Such inappropriate uses would include masturbation, extra-marital sex and sexual relations between two persons of the same sex.

The Church also teaches that artificial contraception violates the moral law. Sexual relations should be the physical expression of our total gift of self. In a contraceptive union that gift cannot be total. It artificially severs the bond between life and love which is part of our nature. The couple withhold their fertility from each other, rendering their union selfish.

---

24 Catechism of the Catholic Church, 2207.

Contraceptive couples use each other to experience sexual pleasure instead of making a compete gift of themselves to each other. Instead of being open to receiving the children sent by God they decide for themselves when they will procreate. And they mistakenly view children as burdens instead of precious gifts sent by God.

Human Life and Sexual Identity

The Christian Tradition holds that, as the Bible teaches, we are created male or female. Our biological sex is a gift from God and intrinsically linked to who we are as people. It is not distinct from our gender identity. Moreover, the Church also teaches that sex is a constituent part of our personhood:

> To be male or female is not just something added to the individual person and so, separable from the rest of the characteristics of a human person. It is intrinsic to the individual, a manner of being and behaving inseparable from the individual person. To be male or female affects not only the biology of the person, but also his/her spirit, culture, social life and all the strata and dimensions of the individual person's life. The human person is either male or female and this particular condition affects the person's entire being.
>
> The difference of sex is obviously present in the genetic configuration of the person as well as in the differentiation of the bodily organs destined for sexual reproduction. But it can also be seen in one's psychological, emotional and cognitive life:
>
> To be male or female does not affect the body alone but also the human spirit because both body and spirit are inseparably united in the one and same person. Unlike the animals, human sexuality modifies also the psychology and the intellectual life of the person. Men and women have differences that affect their way of thinking, acting, perceiving things and of being in the world. There are characteristics proper to women and some proper to men. Moreover, these differences complement each other. Diversity of traits is a source of enrichment for the human person.[25]

In other words, we are either masculine or feminine persons, body and mind or spirit. The internal unity of the human person determines that a man is male in his body and manly in his spirit and a woman is female in her body and womanly in her spirit. Body and spirit are united in one masculine

---

25   John XXIII, *Pacem in Terris*, Encylical letter, Vatican website, April 11, 1963, https://www.vatican.va/content/john-xxiii/en/encyclicals/documents/hf_j-xxiii_enc_11041963_pacem.html, sec. 46.

or feminine person. Hence, every man and woman should acknowledge and accept his or her sexual identity. The Church maintains that transgenderism is a grave moral error.

The Christian Tradition also teaches that human life is sacred from conception to natural death because, from its beginning, it involves the creative action of God and it remains forever in a special relationship with the Creator, who is its sole end. Each human being is made in God's image and likeness. Each one is loved infinitely by God, who alone is the Lord of life from its beginning until its end; no one can under any circumstance claim for himself the right directly to destroy an innocent human being. For this reason, both abortion and euthanasia are considered morally unacceptable.

The State and Society

Like the family, the state is also grounded in natural law and in the divine plan for humanity:

> Since God made men social by nature, and since no society can hold together unless someone be over all, directing all to strive earnestly for the common good, every civilized community must have a ruling authority, and this authority, no less than society itself, has its source in nature, and has, consequently, God for its author.[26]

Catholic Social Teaching holds that the State has a purpose, which is to promote the material and moral prosperity of its citizens. Another way to say this is that the state should promote the common good, which is "the sum total of social conditions that allow people, either as groups or as individuals, to reach their fulfillment more fully and more easily."[27] In sum, the State should seek to create and maintain conditions in the society that make it easy for people to be good.

This common good is not only material but also spiritual, since the members of society are persons with a body and a soul. In fact, the common good is directly linked to the final end of man, which is God, and it therefore has a transcendent dimension. The state cannot pretend to be morally neutral. The State needs to embrace moral values that foster the integral development of its citizens, who, apart from material goods, require many other goods of a spiritual nature: peace, order, justice, freedom, security, etc. The State should consequently promote the exercise of social and civic virtues through which these goods are achieved.

26 John XXIII, *Pacem in Terris*, sec. 46
27 GS, sec. 26.

To do this, the State should enact laws in accordance with the natural law. It must defend true human rights, which are those rights required for us to seek our fulfillment, and would include the right to life, the right to religious freedom, the right to private property, the right to freedom of association, etc. Their ultimate source is not found in the will of the people or the authority of the State, but in the dignity of each human person. It should make laws that promote the stability of the family. It should render justice, protecting the poor from being exploited by the rich.

In fostering the integral development of its citizens, the state should favour the religious dimension of the human person and his transcendent vocation. Specifically, it is important that the state recognize and respect the right to religious freedom. This is much more than freedom of worship. It is the right to live one's life in accordance with one's religious beliefs so long as these do not violate public order.

To ensure the common good, the government has the specific duty to harmonize the claims of different interest groups in society with the requirements of true justice. This is in fact one of the most delicate tasks of public authority: to interpret the common good of the society not only according to the claims of the majority (justice is not determined by majority vote) but also according to the effective good of all the members of the community, including minorities.[28] The government should also respect the principle of subsidiarity, which stipulates that:

> a community of a higher order should not interfere in the internal life of a community of a lower order, depriving the latter of its functions, but rather should support it in case of need and help to co-ordinate its activity with the activities of the rest of society, always with a view to the common good.[29]

So, matters should be handled by the smallest, lowest, or least centralized competent authority. The state should not usurp the role of the family, associations, charities, churches, companies, trade unions, clubs, towns, etc. The state's involvement in areas that belong to these mediating institutions should be temporary and be restricted to circumstances where such involvement is required to deal with situations of injustice that these institutions are incapable of handling. And its involvement should terminate as soon as the situation that required its intervention has been resolved.

28   Pontifical Council for Justice and Peace, *Compendium of the Social Doctrine of the Church*, Roman Curial document, Vatican website, April 2, 2004, sec. 169, https://www.vatican.va/roman_curia/pontifical_councils/justpeace/documents/rc_pc_justpeace_doc_20060526_compendio-dott-soc_en.html#PRESENTATION.
29   Catechism of the Catholic Church, 1883.

This completes our brief look at the Christian worldview as taught by the Catholic Church. We have necessarily had to leave out many aspects of that worldview and have simply concentrated on those that are more in contrast with Expressive Individualism, which we will now go on to examine.

Chapter 2

A New Worldview:
Expressive Individualism and the Modern Self

Introduction

For the past few centuries in Western Europe and North America the predominate Christian worldview has been gradually giving way to a more secularist one. And this process has been speeding up since the 1960s to the point where it is now shared by a sizeable majority of people in the West. Although it tends to defy precise classification, it nevertheless has some defining characteristics that we will examine below. Of course, not all those who hold this worldview will necessarily agree with all the elements that we will ascribe to it. But it is nonetheless true that these attitudes, in a more or less nuanced way, have become the normative way of thinking of a majority of educated urban dwellers in Western Europe and North America.

As we shall see below, in contrast to Christianity, this worldview is humanist in that it places man rather than God squarely at the heart of everything. It takes for its motto the Statement of Protagoras: "Man is the measure of all things." It is also secularist, embracing human reason and ethics and specifically rejecting religious dogma and the supernatural as the basis of morality and decision making. It espouses a kind of philosophical naturalism, which holds that only natural (as opposed to supernatural) forces operate in the world. It shares some characteristics with liberalism in the sense that it considers individual freedom, liberty, autonomy, equality, tolerance, human rights, and the satisfaction of preferences as the key values of political, social, and moral life. It has elements of existentialism and postmodernism in its understanding of how a person's identity is malleable.

It is also rationalist in the sense that it considers reason to be powerful, universal, and reliable and maintains that most problems can be solved by the use of reason. This worldview dominates the mainstream media and major universities. As we will see, people who hold this view consider that most reasonable and educated people will also come to agree with it since it is derived from reason and is therefore more objective than others. They consider other views, including Christianity, to be somehow subjective. What are some of the elements or characteristics of this worldview?

Autonomy, Expressive Individualism, and the Modern Self

As we saw in Chapter 1, a key insight that Christianity contributed to Western Civilization is that all men and women are equal. Christianity holds that each human is a being created in the image and likeness of God, redeemed by the precious blood of Christ, and as such, all men and women are bearers of a profound, inherent, and equal dignity. It contends that everyone, regardless of their religion, is called by God to actualize the full likeness of God imprinted on him at creation by following the Natural Law.

It was this Christian teaching on equality that eventually led to the development of the concept of human rights. However, the Church's teaching on human rights is carefully circumscribed by limits emanating from our human nature and from Natural Law. As we saw in Chapter 1, the natural law is basically those moral principles that set out how we should live if we want to lead happy and fulfilled lives and attain our great potential.

Since following the Natural Law is what allows each person to thrive, then each person has a human right to act according to the Natural Law. So, in the Christian Tradition, true human rights are linked to the Natural Law and the only human rights that exist are those that allow someone to follow the Natural Law. One cannot arbitrarily invent new human rights unrelated to Natural Law. The modern understanding of autonomy retains the Christian insight that all men and women are equal and each one possesses an inherent dignity. However, it has rejected the Church's foundation for this teaching. It no longer believes that there is a universal human nature or a natural law that should be obeyed.

This notion of autonomy is linked to a new understanding of the Self, which has come to mean more than a basic level of self-awareness. For the modern self, there is a decisive emphasis on inwardness. My interior psychological convictions, how I understand myself with respect to others, and my milieu essentially constitute my identity: who I am. In order to understand my identity and the purpose of my life, I should give priority to my inner psychology, my feelings, and my intuition. And to be happy and to find fulfillment in life, I must be true to my inner self, to my identity, and so engage in activities that bring me psychological well-being.[1]

In order to refer to this new understanding of the self, Robert Bellah coined the term *Expressive Individualism*, which he defined as follows: "Expressive individualism holds that each person has a unique core of feeling and intuition that should unfold or be expressed if individuality is to be realized."[2] It accordingly holds that each person is free to create or forge his own identity. In

---

1   For this chapter, I am heavily indebted to Carl Trueman, *The Rise and Triumph of the Modern Self* (Wheaton: Crossway, 2020), Chapter 1: Reimagining the Self.

2   Robert N. Bellah et al, *Habits of the Heart: Individualism and Commitment in American Life* (Berkely: University of California Press, 1996), 333-334.

order to lead an authentic life and be true to himself, each one should express outwardly what he feels inwardly.

Charles Taylor has defined the culture of authenticity as:

> One where each one of us has his/her own way of realizing her humanity, and that it is important to find and live out one's own, as against surrendering to conformity with a model imposed on us from outside, by society, or the previous generation, or religious or political authority.[3]

This autonomy is considered to be an essential characteristic of personhood, to the point that one's dignity lies in being an autonomous human being who can choose his own values, his own way of life, and create his own identity. This individualism leads to what is referred to as the *Autonomous Self*. For the autonomous self, human nature is considered to be very malleable. As Jean-Paul Sartre said:

> What is meant… by saying that existence precedes essence? It means first of all, man exists, turns up, appears on the scene, and, only afterwards, defines himself. If man, as the existentialist conceives him, is indefinable, it is because at first, he is nothing. Only afterward will he be something, and he himself will have made what he will be."[4]

A version of this view, known as popular existentialism, holds that identity is something people construct and reconstruct freely, and each construction deserves equal affirmation, with law and social custom ensuring that all identities are respected and affirmed. This autonomy means self-definition: each individual has the right to decide his own values and his own meaning of life, and neither the State nor anyone else should interfere with his right to pursue that vision and to lead the life he chooses. The only condition is that he not interfere with the preferences of others and does not cause harm to others (the Do No Harm principle). Therefore, all ways of life that do not harm others are equally acceptable and must not be criticized.

This does not mean, of course, that one forges one's identity in a vacuum. In the 1980s, some feminist philosophers proposed a relational conception of the self, emphasizing the importance of relationships and social context in shaping our identities. They held that our sense of self is not formed in isolation but is deeply linked to our interactions and connections with others. They pointed out that our identities are significantly shaped by our relationships with other individuals and with communities and institutions. These relationships deeply

---

3   Charles Taylor, *A Secular Age* (Cambridge: Belknap, 2007), 475.
4   Jean-Paul Sartre, *Existentialism is a Humanism*, trans. Carol Macomber (New Haven: Yale University Press, 2007).

influence our worldview and provide a framework through which we understand ourselves and others. So, for these philosophers, each identity is necessarily forged through interdependence and connection with others. Yet, although these relationships clearly do condition our ability to shape our identity, the basic fact remains: within the limits imposed by our background, experiences, and relationships, each one is free to shape his identity as he wishes, and his choices must be above reproach.

It is obvious that, for most people, someone who spends his life serving the needy and giving of himself to make the world a better place would be viewed more positively than someone who does not help others and engages mainly in self-gratification. But the latter lifestyle cannot be distinguished from the former in terms of some sort of objective norm of good and evil, and it would be considered intolerant to criticize it. The only limit to what one can choose is the autonomy of others, whose free choices must be respected.

Hence, it makes perfect sense for those who espouse the modern notion of the self to exercise autonomy by, for example, choosing to adopt the gender they feel best corresponds to them sexually and emotionally, or deciding to end their life through euthanasia, or terminating a pregnancy, or divorcing a spouse, or embracing the sexual orientation they feel most comfortable with, etc. Since for those who hold this worldview, one only possesses personhood and dignity if one has autonomy and consciousness, a fetus is not considered to be a person and so is not a subject of human rights.[5] It is true that most legal systems do forbid late-stage abortions, but for Expressive Individualism, the law should not prevent the mother from exercising her autonomy and aborting her fetus. Even though one may be personally against abortion, there is a need to respect the autonomy of the expecting mother and not impose one's personal views on her if she wishes to undergo an abortion. Apart from the Do No Harm Principle, this autonomy is considered absolute. No one may impose a moral law on another nor stipulate for him the meaning and purpose of his life or of the universe, since that would not leave him free to decide those matters on his own. Those who embrace Expressive Individualism hold, of course, that there is an objective natural order in the universe in the sense that matter is subject to the laws of physics. But apart from this, they hold that no universal, objective moral order can be found or admitted either in the cosmos or in human beings. The world is essentially a product of chance.

In order for society to function well, we follow the Do No Harm Principle and the Golden Rule (treat others as you would wish them to treat you). But these are not part of an objective moral order. Indeed, we are not bound by any reality other than the laws of physics. We are not bound by any natural moral

---

5 Carl Trueman, *Strange New World* (Wheaton: Crossway, 2022), 150-151.

law. If we were, we would not be free to make ourselves into whatever we want to be, since the natural law would limit and constrain us, obliging us to adopt certain forms of behaviour that might conflict with the identity that we feel moved to assume.

Since there is no Natural Law, the only "meaning" in the universe is the meaning we each give it. It is true that many of those who hold to expressive individualism find meaning by embracing spiritual values and seek to lead their lives by them. But they would never maintain that those values should be held by others. So, there is no need for my meaning to be the same as yours. Hence, outside of what science can tell us, there is no need to have a common view of what the universe is. To impose such a view would be a threat to our freedom to be what we choose. As U.S. Supreme Court Justice Anthony Kennedy famously put it in Planned Parenthood vs. Casey, "At the heart of liberty is the right to define one's own concept of existence, of meaning, of the universe, and of the mystery of human life."[6]

In order to respect the autonomy of each individual, the State should refrain from imposing or endorsing any particular conception of the good life or of what gives value to life. It can only enforce the *Do No Harm* principle. As Canadian Supreme Court Justice Wilson put it in Morgentaler v. the Queen (1988),

> The rights guaranteed in the Charter erect around the individual an invisible fence over which the State will not be allowed to trespass. The basic theory underlying the Charter is that the State will respect choices made by individuals and, to the greatest extent possible, will avoid subordinating these choices to any one conception of the good life.[7]

A state violates the autonomy of its citizens if it upholds a version of the good that subverts an individual's autonomous choice. So, the State must enforce the Do No Harm Principle, but in all else it should remain neutral with respect to values. So, the Modern Self is not to be subject to anyone unless he voluntarily accepts that person's authority (governmental authorities, one's boss at work, etc.). No one can legitimately claim to have authority over us without our consent. There is no higher law above human laws that we need to obey, other than the laws of physics. We should not allow our actions to be directed by any god, church, or religion. Throughout history, personal autonomy has been restricted by traditional hierarchies and religious teachings often based on superstition and irrational beliefs. These must now be cast off.

In 1968, there were massive student revolts and demonstrations in France and Germany. Their slogan was "Il est interdit d'interdire," which means "it is

---

6   Planned Parenthood of Southeastern Pa. v. Casey, 505 U.S. 833, 851 (1992).
7   R. v. Morgentaler, [1988] 1 S.C.R. 30.

forbidden to forbid," which perfectly encapsulates Expressive Individualism's stance on autonomy and which could well serve as a slogan for Expressive Individualism as a whole.[8] As Noam Chomsky, put it:

> I think it only makes sense to seek out and identify structures of authority, hierarchy, and domination in every aspect of life, and to challenge them; unless a justification for them can be given, they are illegitimate, and should be dismantled, to increase the scope of human freedom.[9]

The Modern Self demands that society recognize and affirm its choices. Indeed, criticizing someone's personal lifestyle choice is seen not only as a sign of one's disapproval of the behaviour in question, but as a personal attack on the individual, since it calls into question his very dignity and his right to forge his own identity. In modern jargon, this is referred to as respect for diversity and inclusion.

The one limitation that is accepted is the Do No Harm principle: my choices must not cause harm to others. One can live out one's concept of the good life provided he does not harm anyone else. And harm is not considered to be just physical, financial, or moral harm but includes anything that would prevent someone else from living out his values, from engaging in his chosen lifestyle, or from leading the life of his choice, and would also include disrespecting another's lifestyle.

The Do No Harm Principle is not considered a natural law in the sense of being a principle of morality that is derived from our human nature. As we shall see below when we discuss morality, the Do No Harm Principle is rather the result of a social consensus, since it is a requirement for people to live in peace with one another under a social contract. It is a political and social construct rather than a natural law. John Stuart Mill, one of the principal architects of this position, stated it as follows:

> The only freedom which deserves the name, is that of pursuing our own good in our own way, so long as we do not attempt to deprive others of theirs, or impede their efforts to obtain it. Each is the proper guardian of his own health, whether bodily, or mental and spiritual. Mankind are greater gainers by suffering each other to live as seems good to themselves, than by compelling each to live as seems good to the rest.[10]

8 Melissa McCaffrey, "Il est interdit d'interdire! (It is forbidden to forbid): The Protests That Defined a Generation," Recto Verso, May 16, 2018, https://www.rectoversoblog.com/2018/05/16/il-est-interdit-dinterdire-it-is-forbidden-to-forbid-the-protests-that-defined-a-generation/.

9 Interview done for Red and Black Revolution [Issue No. 2, 1995], conducted in May 1995 by Kevin Doyle.

10 John Stuart Mill, On Liberty (London: John W. Parker And Son, 1859), 13.

The autonomous individual will normally also adhere to the Golden Rule and would even go beyond this. The majority value love and peace and seek to practice empathy, service, and compassion, to be kind and generous, and to help those in need. They sincerely work towards the elimination of disease, ignorance, and poverty and to making the world a better place. In contrast to the Christian worldview, Expressive Individualism considers the individual (rather than the family) as the fundamental cell of society, foundational to all human associations that make up a civilization. It certainly values the family but considers that the dictates of personal autonomy are such that the individual's interests must take precedence.

Morality, Moral Relativism and Affirmation[11]

The autonomous individual considers morality to be man-made. There is no authority above man. There is no natural moral law that flows necessarily from our nature. If we choose to follow the Golden Rule and the Do No Harm principle, it is so that we can live together in peace and security. As we saw in Chapter One, for a Christian, the moral law is written on the human heart, and one discovers it. For the Modern Self, man is the source and author of the moral law by the use of his reason alone. He does not discover it, he creates it, a position that is referred to as moral relativism.[12]

Essentially, we see that we need to have laws to live by or we will have chaos. So, the basis for morals is a social agreement or social contract. We agree with everyone else not to exercise our autonomy in a way that conflicts with their autonomy. As a society develops, a certain consensus on moral questions takes shape that considers immoral any conduct that harms others. This consensus, usually referred to as Public Reason, becomes the foundation for its laws. Such laws, in turn, become the only external criteria of morality for citizens. Each one may do as he likes as long as he doesn't break the law and respects the two basic ethical principles. Hence, the law is not based on any truth other than Public Reason. As we become more enlightened, the social consensus changes, and so the law will change and the moral criteria valid for that time and place will change too. Examples of laws that have changed with the social consensus would include those that allowed slavery and laws that forbade abortion, cannabis, euthanasia, inter-racial marriage, etc. Hence, for the relativist, morality is evolving and socially constructed.

11   This discussion on moral relativism and tolerance is based on the article: "The Four Cardinal Virtues of Secularism," Catholic Legate, October 5, 2020, https://www.catholic-legate.org/post/the-four-cardinal-virtues-of-secularism.

12   For a study of moral relativism, see: Chris Gowans, "Moral Relativism," in *Stanford Encyclopedia of Philosophy* (Stanford University: Spring, 2021), https://plato.stanford.edu/entries/moral-relativism/.

As we saw above, one is free to do whatever one wishes so long as he doesn't harm others. The autonomy of others and their choices must be respected, and hence tolerance takes on great importance. However, for the Modern Self, the notion of tolerance has become unacceptable, since it implies that one is putting up with conduct that is in some way inferior or reprehensible. Instead of simply tolerating the behaviour of others, we should affirm and celebrate the different identities that people feel moved to forge. For example, many historically oppressed minorities have now won the right and freedom to publicly express their identity. This is a cause for rejoicing and an opportunity to display solidarity and encouragement.

Respecting the rights of others means affirming their choices and behaviour. One cannot condemn anyone's behaviour as long as it does not harm anyone else, since there is no basis on which to do so. And this affirmation extends not just to behavior, but also to their beliefs and truth claims.

As we saw in Chapter 1, for the Christian there is a natural law, and its principles are universal, objective, and absolute. In Expressive Individualism, on the other hand, since man makes the moral law, he may accordingly change it as his situation changes. The social consensus at the moment dictates that we follow the Golden Rule and the Do No Harm principle. But these are not moral absolutes and are subject to change. Hence, there are no moral absolutes, no natural law, no objective moral norms, and no universal moral values that we simply discover. Each one should choose his or her own values and his or her own truth. And everyone should respect and affirm the choice of values others make.

The fact that there are differing understandings as to what constitutes the good life means that Expressive Individualism with its moral relativism must be adopted for the sake of social peace and to ensure fairness, justice, equality, and human rights. It observes matters from a neutral and superior position that enables it to supervise other views without changing them. This moral relativism that is so appealing and attractive seems necessary for a free society to flourish:

1. It is open-minded and respectful of different views and opinions. It allows for a diversity of lifestyles (common-law unions, divorced and remarried couples, same-sex couples, multiple partner unions, etc.), and so is a source of richness for a society and for the individual. This diversity increases the range of available options without forcing any of them on anyone. So, more options translate into more freedom.

2. It is a practical way to live in a multicultural and pluralistic society and to ensure peace, fairness, justice, equality, and human rights in society. Since controversial moral issues divide citizens and cause civil discontent, the State should remove those issues from the political process.

3. It guarantees individual freedom: people can do what they want. It allows each one to exercise autonomy with respect to issues like divorce, abortion, same-sex relationships, contraception, euthanasia, transgenderism, promiscuity, consumption of drugs, etc.
4. It prevents religious institutions from controlling the lives of people who don't agree with their teachings.
5. It is a mature and critical minded position with regards to authority and convention. It allows each person to think for himself: "I will decide what is right and wrong for me."

On the other hand, Christian teaching on morality, which seems to impose moral values on everyone, is seen as:

1. Narrow-minded, judgmental, and intolerant.
2. Arrogant and dogmatic, as though only the Church has the truth.
3. Anti-democratic, since it denies that the values espoused by the majority should prevail.
4. Hypocritical and corrupt, for example, in light of the sexual abuse of minors by priests and the ensuing cover-up, the abuse of indigenous youth in the residential schools, etc.

Christians are seen as lacking the maturity and boldness to think for themselves. They have relinquished this freedom and simply act as the Church tells them to act.

Human Rights and Equality

This understanding of autonomy gives rise to a specific understanding of human rights and equality. In terms of human rights, it holds that each person has the right to life, liberty, and the pursuit of happiness. Included in these last two categories is the human right to pursue one's own life project in the measure that it does not harm others. Hence, a person can claim that he has a human right to do anything that is needed to pursue his life project. In enforcing this concept, the courts have granted a right to abortion, to euthanasia, to same-sex marriage, etc. Equality requires that everyone's choices and acts will be treated equally by the law and before the courts. In law, this is usually referred to as substantive equal protection. This right to equality or to equal treatment before the law is one of the most central of all the rights, and the courts will generally favour it over any other claim that appears to conflict with it.

The precise meaning of equality, however, is not always clear. Does it mean equality of opportunity or of outcome? In other words, does it mean that everyone should have the same opportunity to succeed, thereby allowing those who are more talented or fortunate, or who work harder to better their condition, or should there be a system in place to ensure that everyone benefits equally regardless of talent, merit, or effort? And if the former, can it really be said that those who have been historically disadvantaged and discriminated against have the same opportunity as those who have not so suffered? Should there be some system in place to privilege such people, through affirmative action, for example?

It is generally understood that, in order for there to be equality, there must first be equity, a levelling of the playing field. To give everyone the same opportunity, it is necessary to implement some form of affirmative action in order to at least partially redress historic wrongs. The notion of Equality is usually accompanied by those of Diversity and Inclusion. Essentially, the Expressive Individualist will embrace, support, and accept people of all racial, sexual, gender, religious, and socioeconomic backgrounds.[13]

Secularity

The Modern Self, or autonomous individual, can be an atheist who believes that God does not exist. Or he can be an agnostic, who neither affirms nor denies the existence of God but rather holds that there is not enough evidence to be sure that he exists, which usually results in practical atheism. Or he can be a deist, who believes that a god exists and created the world, but, having created it, he leaves it to follow its own course and does not intervene in any way.

He may also believe in a type of Eastern Mysticism, pantheism, New Age Philosophy, etc. In these cases, he will often hold that there is a natural order in the universe and that things happen for a reason. This is sometimes expressed by the notion of karma, balance in the universe, etc. He may believe that one can tap into one's spiritual side and direct the flow of spiritual energy to others. He will often also believe in what is referred to as The Source. Some hold that The Source is simply the spiritual side of man, while others believe it is the universe itself. Still others believe that it is an entity distinct from ourselves. This is a vast and complex subject, and we cannot even begin to do it justice.

In some cases, the autonomous individual may even consider himself spiritual but not religious, perhaps believing in the existence of a personal god with whom he has a personal relationship, to whom he prays, from whom he seeks guidance, and to whom he gives thanks. But in none of these cases will he subscribe to any organized religion that will impose on him a set of beliefs and a moral code.

---

13   Lisa Dunn, "What Is Diversity, Equity & Inclusion (DEI)," *Inclusion Hub*, November 6, 2020, https://www.inclusionhub.com/articles/what-is-dei.

For the Modern Self, organized religion as a set of practices or way of life is seen as outmoded. It "is quaint, antiquated, logically indefensible, has historically produced ignorance and misplaced sectarian belligerency and oppression, and has been steadily disintegrating under the irresistible advances of the Enlightenment and the triumphant march of science for at least 500 years."[14] But organized religion is accepted, at least at the personal level, because everyone is free to do/believe what he wants. As we saw, respect for autonomy is one of the central tenets of Expressive Individualism. So, if religion fulfills some emotional need for someone, then he is free to go ahead and worship. But religion and religiously based values must not be imposed on anyone, so they must be excluded from public life.[15]

Reason

In this worldview, reason is understood to be the ability to know truth using the natural powers of our mind without need of any divine revelation or religious superstition. People obviously also rely on intuition and their inner voice in their daily lives and tend to follow their conscience. But they consider that reason is powerful and reliable and that most problems can be solved by the use of reason. Hence, we do not need faith to build civilization. It is by reason using science that man has conquered nature, made scientific and technological breakthroughs, increased life expectancy, improved health, and raised the standard of living. This confidence in reason means that one should adopt a critical stance towards customs or traditions that seem incompatible with reason. They need to be examined in the light of reason to verify whether they in fact serve a positive or rational purpose and contribute to a better society or not. Customs and traditions that do not meet this test can be discarded. Furthermore, since this worldview has been arrived at using reason and is based largely on reason, those who oppose it are seen as not acting rationally.

This confidence in reason has been somewhat undermined by postmodernism. Postmodernism is a complicated and elaborate philosophy that is beyond our scope to explain in detail.[16] Suffice it to say that it adopts moral relativism and a skeptical attitude as regards the ability of our reason

---

14   Conrad Black, "By debasing religion, Canadian Intellectuals are playing a dangerous game", *National Post*, Feb 19, 2021, https://nationalpost.com/opinion/conrad-black-by-debasing-religion-canadian-intellectuals-are-playing-a-dangerous-game.

15   For a discussion of Laicism, see "Laicism," *New Catholic Encyclopedia*, Encyclopedia.com, (July 26, 2023), https://www.encyclopedia.com/religion/encyclopedias-almanacs-transcripts-and-maps/laicism.

16   For a study of postmodernism, see: Gary Aylesworth, "Postmodernism," in *Stanford Encyclopedia of Philosophy*, (Stanford University: Spring, 2015), https://plato.stanford.edu/entries/postmodernism/.

to know reality. It maintains that all our knowledge of reality is affected by our viewpoint, by our background and the circumstances in which we live, by the political, historical, or cultural discourses to which we have been exposed, by ideology, etc. and so there can be no objective, rational knowledge. It maintains that reality is itself a mental construct.

We can see that this post-modern philosophy has had an effect on the evolution of Expressive Individualism, which has itself adopted moral relativism, and which claims that each one's nature and personal identity is not something objective but can be defined and re-defined at the initiative of each individual. This skepticism as regards our ability to know truth also insinuates itself into other aspects of life. However, the more extreme post-modernist skepticism as regards reason's ability to understand reality is mostly confined to the academy. In their day to day lives, most people, whether they embrace Expressive Individualism or not, maintain a healthy trust in their ability to grasp reality and to know the truth.

Scientific Materialism

The autonomous individual will normally embrace practical materialism, which is the belief that the only thing that counts in our understanding of the universe is the material stuff of the universe and what has arisen from that. It is true; as we mentioned above, some also believe in a natural order to the cosmos, karma, balance in the universe, etc. Many also hold that there is a spiritual side to man and believe in the existence of a spiritual realm of some sort. But this spiritual realm is seen as a natural phenomenon rather than supernatural. It is distinct from and has nothing to do with the Christian belief in a personal, transcendent God who intervenes in our lives. Some may also believe in an afterlife or in a form of reincarnation. But they will usually hold that we can't know anything certain about these possibilities, so they are irrelevant to this life.

The practical materialist contends that all we can know with certainty is that which we can observe scientifically. He holds that belief in an afterlife can be useful if it moves people to lead good lives and gives them psychological benefits, but it can be harmful if it causes violence or diverts people's attention and efforts away from improving the lot of humanity in this life. For example, if they were truly enlightened, monks in a cloistered monastery would be fighting disease, poverty, and violence instead of praying all day. Enlightenment is the process by which people come to see that religion and other primitive forms of knowledge are now outmoded. And so they reject them and come to embrace science. This is considered one of the great goals of education. Although each person is free to choose the meaning and values of his life and to pursue his own life project, the enlightened person acts with a view to this life only.

According to scientific materialism, everything acts according to the laws of nature. No exceptions are possible, and so there can be no miracles. Apparent miracles can always be explained scientifically. Everything about us can be explained by the matter out of which we are made. Evolution is the process by which present day beings have arisen from the original stuff (atoms, molecules, subatomic particles, energy, etc.) of the universe. For example, we are witnessing a great effort in the scientific community to explain our behaviour through our genes.

If the material universe can only be understood by studying matter, then the science that studies matter becomes the surest source of knowledge. One can only truly know something with certainty if it can be proven scientifically. Science uses the empirical method by which it carries out objective observations by eye and by instrument. It builds models or hypotheses to account for the observed phenomena. It then tests the hypotheses by deducing consequences and seeing whether they can be verified or falsified by experiment. All material phenomena are presumed to be explicable by reference to material bodies and forces. Science discovers objective truth and yields facts that are true for all.[17]

This empirical method is thought to be the gold standard of evidence, and the further something is from this method, the less reflective of objective reality it is taken to be. So, any truth claim not supportable by the methods of empirical science is weak in some way. And since the claims of Christian theology and ethics cannot be the object of a verifiable hypothesis tested by the scientific method, they cannot count as genuine knowledge and are not worthy of rational belief. Since what faith teaches contradicts what we know by our reason and by science, both cannot be true. It holds that Christians fail to sufficiently trust reason's power to know truth. It also contends that science, using reason, has explained many phenomena that more primitive people ascribed to the gods and that at one point everything will be explainable by reason and science. For example, primitive people thought that storms, lightning, and thunder were caused by the anger of the gods. Now we know this not to be true. Furthermore, Darwin has shown how man evolved, and so we know that man was not created in the way that the Book of Genesis describes. In addition, astronomy, through the Big Bang theory, has shown that the Genesis story of Creation is not true. Geology has shown that the world is millions of years old, not just 6,000, as the Bible says. Freud has explained our passions and desires, so we no longer have to posit the existence of a devil to tempt us. Science has replaced God as the ultimate authority.[18]

17   This position is referred to as Scientism: "Scientism," *Wikimedia Foundation*, July 9, 2023, https://en.wikipedia.org/wiki/Scientism.

18   For a study of scientific materialism, see: "Scientific Materialism," American History Through Literature 1870-1920, Encyclopedia.com, July 25, 2023, https://www.encyclopedia.com.

It is true that there is some mistrust as regards vaccines, genetically modified foods, etc. And many people fear that technology is being used to manipulate and control us. Yet, in spite of this growing mistrust, for the Modern Self, the value and validity of science is thought to be demonstrated by the progress in technology and medicine that it has produced. Man conquers nature, harnessing natural forces to his own needs and desires, overcoming natural disasters like plague, famine and floods that used to devastate societies. For example, through science, medicine has extended life-spans, lowered infant mortality, raised the quality of life, eradicated certain diseases, etc.

Apart from empirical science, knowledge derived from reason also includes philosophy, which is the study of such fundamental issues as essence and existence, the nature of reality, knowledge, truth, ethics, beauty, language, etc. Knowledge derived from reason also includes the social sciences (sociology, anthropology, psychology, economics, political science, linguistics, etc.) and other paths to knowledge that do not rely on religious faith. Yet, knowledge derived from philosophy and the social sciences, though valid, is judged to be not as certain as that obtained from the natural sciences. Of course, it is undeniable that there are many things that we hold as true even though they are not subject to empirical proof. These would include historical facts certainly, but also other things that we know to exist, such as love, friendship, integrity, etc. These are referred to as subjective truths.

Progress

A basic tenet of this worldview is that humanity achieves progress through time and that, as a result of evolutionary forces, history is moving unstoppably towards a better world.[19] Yes, there is the occasional hiccup, such as the 20th century's world wars and murderous regimes, but those are considered to be only temporary detours in the march of progress. So, as part of the social contract, we should all work to aid this process. It holds that, as time goes by, human life improves: knowledge grows and conditions of life improve, primarily through technology and education.

It is clear that this progress comes about through human effort rather than through any sort of divine assistance or divine providence. We should not look to God to solve any of our problems. People did that in the past out of ignorance; now we know better. As mentioned, those who hold to New Age Philosophy or some sort of Eastern Mysticism do try to tap into the spiritual realm, seeking to

---

19 Steven Wall, "Perfectionism in Moral and Political Philosophy," in *Stanford Encyclopedia of Philosophy*, (Stanford University: Fall, 2021), https://plato.stanford.edu/entries/perfectionism-moral/.

send positive energy and loving thoughts to others. Some people who embrace Expressive Individualism consider themselves spiritual, though not religious, and pray to a personal god for guidance. But the great engine of progress is considered to be science and technology. We become masters of nature through science. More food, better fuel, control of natural disasters, and especially medicine, which improves our health, wipes out disease, and increases longevity.

The biggest obstacle to progress is religious superstition and traditional conservative values and customs. For example, in his book, *Why I Am Not a Christian*, Bertrand Russell, a famous atheist and a secular liberal who promoted a lifestyle based on autonomy rather than the natural moral law, had this to say about progress and religion:

> I say quite deliberately that the Christian religion, as organized in its Churches, has been and still is the principal enemy of moral progress in the world.
>
> The knowledge exists by which universal happiness can be secured; the chief obstacle to its utilization for that purpose is the teaching of religion. Religion prevents our children from having a rational education; religion prevents us from removing the fundamental causes of war; religion prevents us from teaching the ethic of scientific cooperation in place of the old fierce doctrines of sin and punishment. It is possible that mankind is on the threshold of a golden age; but, if so, it will be necessary first to slay the dragon that guards the door, and this dragon is religion.[20]

In this passage, Bertrand Russell refers to a coming golden age. This is the secular utopia, the paradise that the autonomous individual expects will come about as a result of the victory of Expressive Individualism with its emphasis on autonomy, equality, freedom, moral relativism, and human rights.

The State

Since we have to live together, we form a society and a government and enter into a social agreement or social contract. The State does not have any authority over us except what we give it. However, since different people have desires and life projects that conflict with each other, the State must have sufficient authority to settle such conflicts in order to keep people from harming each other and to ensure peace, justice, equality, human rights, etc. In order to carry out this mission, the State can exercise power over its citizens, even against their will.

20　Bertrand Russell, *Why I am Not a Christian and Other Essays on Religion and Related Subjects* (Abingdon-on-Thames: Routledge, 1996), 17.

This power of the government to settle conflicts and impose peace brooks no opposition. The power of the State stems from the wills of the citizens who wish to protect their right to pursue their life projects. The purpose of the government is to protect the rights its citizens have elected it to protect and to ensure justice, equality, etc. In order to guarantee equality, the government should engage in the redistribution of wealth, institute socialized health care for all, establish a social safety net for those who need it, etc. and has authority to oblige the citizens to pay taxes to finance these programs.

Government should be democratic, because each person should have a say in how they are governed, since this is part of autonomy. Any form of government that is not democratic risks becoming tyrannical, even if it is benign.

Conclusion

For the Modern Self, who we are, the values we espouse, how we lead our lives, the way we express our sexuality, the activities we engage in for pleasure or purpose, etc., are purely matters of personal choice. No third party may dictate moral rules on these subjects that would impugn one's choices so long as we respect the Do No Harm principle and the Golden Rule. Directly opposed to this is the Catholic Church's teaching on the human person, sexuality, and the nature of the family. The single biggest obstacle to the establishment of a secularist paradise is Catholic moral teaching on these issues.

The ethics of Expressive Individualism align with Christian moral teaching on issues like murder, rape, theft, and terrorism, just as they accord with the Do No Harm principle outlined above. But it opposes Christianity's teachings on the human person, sexuality, and the nature of the family.

The second biggest obstacle to its agenda and to the establishment of a secular utopia is the traditional Christian family, which passes on Christian piety, the Christian worldview, and traditional moral teaching to the children. Through their upbringing, these children tend to trust their family over the State, and so are resistant to Expressive Individualism. Many of them risk becoming as intolerant and dogmatic as their parents and will not become autonomous individuals who can think for themselves. Thus, Expressive Individualism opposes teachings that would restrict freedom of choice and seeks to liberate the traditional family from the constraints imposed on it by that traditional model. It seeks to do this by promoting state control of education as well as freedom of choice in such areas as contraception, no-fault divorce, access to abortion services, same-sex marriage, transgenderism, free love, etc., since these ensure people's autonomy.

Chapter 3

Comparing the Two Worldviews

From this brief look at the two worldviews, it is evident that they are incompatible. The underlying theme illustrating the stark contrast between them can be illustrated by the Christian emphasis on purpose and Expressive Individualism's emphasis on autonomy. Christianity teaches that the world was created from nothing by an all-good, personal God who loves us and answers our prayers. He has a purpose and plan for mankind and continues to watch over humanity with his divine providence, and that fact bestows purpose on everything. On the other hand, Expressive Individualism contends that neither the universe nor man has any god-given purpose. Our life has the purpose that we give it. Even if it is possible that a personal god exists, he is not concerned with what happens to us on earth, so there is no sense in looking to him for any guidance, assistance, etc. We and the universe are the products of chance. Each man is autonomous and has to decide for himself what meaning and purpose he will give to his life and to the universe. We are on our own and must make our own way in this world, exercising our autonomy. This contrast can be more specifically illustrated in the following eight points:

1. Christianity teaches that, in accordance with his plan for mankind, God has given each person a human nature. We do not decide what our human nature is. We rather discover it. For the autonomous individual, our human nature is considered malleable. Each one can exercise his autonomy by constructing and re-constructing his nature and his identity over time.

2. Christianity teaches that there is a natural, moral law. It consists of those principles that indicate how we should lead our lives if we want to flourish and be happy in this life and the next. Since it is based on our human nature and on our purpose, which do not change, the natural moral law is absolute, objective, and universal. It cannot be relative or subjective. For the Modern Self, there is no god-given purpose to our life. Each one must decide the purpose of his life for himself. In addition, since our human nature is malleable, there can be no absolute, objective, and universal moral law. The only moral principles that are firm are the Golden Rule and the Do No Harm principle. And, as we have seen and as Nietzsche pointed out, even these two principles can be subject to change in the future since Expressive Individualism cannot provide

a rationale for them. Apart from those two principles, morality is relative. Each one must decide for himself what moral and ethical rules he wishes to follow.

3. Christianity teaches that our sexuality has a purpose; and in accordance with that purpose the sexual act should only take place in the context of a permanent and exclusive commitment of a man and a woman to each other, which we call marriage. The Church considers extra-marital sex, sexual relations between two persons of the same sex, divorce and artificial contraception to be grave moral errors. Expressive individualism, on the other hand, firmly upholds personal autonomy. This autonomy means self-definition: each individual has the right to decide his own values, his own meaning of life, and the meaning of his own sexuality. Neither the state nor any religious authority, nor anyone else may interfere with his right to pursue that vision and lead the life he chooses. Hence, the autonomous individual contends that he has a perfect right to exercise his autonomy by engaging in extra marital sex, in sexual relations with someone of the same sex, in using contraception, or by divorcing his or her spouse.

4. In the Christian tradition, our body and, therefore, our biological sex are intrinsically linked to who we are as people. The sexualized body is a gift from God and essentially bound up with God's plan and purpose for us to multiply. Our biological sex is not distinct from our gender identity. So, transgenderism is considered a grave moral error. The autonomous individual, on the other hand, holds that it makes perfect sense for people to exercise their autonomy by choosing to adopt the gender they feel best corresponds to them sexually and emotionally.

5. Christianity teaches that human life is sacred from conception to natural death. No one may, under any circumstance, claim for himself the right directly to destroy an innocent human being. For this reason, both abortion and euthanasia are considered morally unacceptable. Expressive individualism's belief in personal autonomy means that one has a perfect right to end one's life whenever one wishes. And since one only possesses personhood and dignity if one has autonomy and self-consciousness, a fetus is not fully a person and so cannot benefit from the right to life.

6. Christianity teaches that we are all fallen creatures prone to sin. We each have within us a deep source of iniquity. So, although with the grace of God we have a great potential to lead fulfilling, happy, and holy lives and are called to act as salt, light, and leaven in the heart of society, it is a mistake to expect to create heaven on earth. We should strive for progress and work towards making the best society possible, but always remember that the human condition renders the perfect society impossible. We are wayfarers on our way to our true homeland in heaven. Expressive Individualism holds, on

the other hand, that there is no inherent limit to human progress. Through science, technology, and reason, mankind can create a prosperous society free from religious superstition and conservative values, characterized by peace, justice, freedom, equality, and tolerance. This is the Golden Age prophesized by Bertrand Russell, the paradise that the autonomous individual aims at.

7. Christianity maintains that it is possible for man with his mind to know the truth about reality. With our rationality, through abstract reasoning, it is possible to know the essence or nature of an object. Because of this, man can objectively know something about God, himself and the world. He is able to understand human nature and so arrive at a knowledge of the natural law and so of ethics. He is able to know good from evil in an objective way. This position (called moderate realism in Philosophy) was held by Aristotle and expounded by Thomas Aquinas. By the end of the Middle Ages, it was the standard or generally accepted position throughout Europe and remained so until the mid-Twentieth Century. Expressive Individualism denies that we are able to know the true nature of objects. It maintains that we are limited to knowing appearances or phenomena. Through observation and experimentation, empirical science is able to provide us with the practical knowledge of reality, which is all that we really need to make progress.

8. Christianity teaches that, although we have feelings, emotions, and sentiments, we should accept the objective facts about our human nature and external reality and conform our inner feelings to that objective reality. Expressive Individualism holds the opposite position. It contends that our interior, psychological life, and beliefs must be given priority, to which external reality must conform.

How Did Expressive Individualism Displace Christianity?

By the end of the Middle Ages, the Christian worldview was so firmly entrenched in European culture and in the minds of Europeans that it appeared to be unassailable. The proofs for the existence of God were essentially irrefutable once one accepted basic Aristotelian-Thomistic philosophy. The Christian understanding of man, original sin, and redemption constituted the only complete and satisfactory explanation of the human condition on offer. Its understanding of the purpose of human existence, together with its demanding and elevated moral teaching, provided a clear, ethical roadmap to every baptized person. How then did it happen that this edifice was little by little undermined and replaced by Expressive Individualism in the popular mind over the ensuing centuries? Libraries have been written on this subject. Here it will suffice to provide some of the highlights.

Original sin is the sin of all ages. Like Adam and Eve, man is always tempted to mistakenly see the moral law as a restriction and to understand freedom in terms of autonomy, as freedom from apparent constraints instead of freedom for growth in virtue. This tendency is part of our fallen human nature. This has led man to want to break free from the moral law and from what he sees as the control of the Church and constitutes an important element in the displacing of the Christian worldview.

As Larry Siedentop has shown,[1] Christianity essentially invented the individual. In the ancient world, people understood society as a collection of extended families (clans, tribes). Each family had its own gods and worshipped its ancestors. The whole of society was based on the clan, hierarchy, and a natural inequality. Christianity introduced the notion of moral equality and imbedded it into European culture and civilization. It taught that each man and woman is created in the image and likeness of God, redeemed by Christ, and called to a transcendent destiny. As such, each man and woman, regardless of social status, possesses a profound, inherent, and equal dignity. Each man and woman is called by God to actualize the full likeness of God imprinted on them at creation by following the Natural Law. Little by little, over the centuries, Christianity also introduced social equality into European culture. It insisted that it was not sufficient to pay lip service to moral equality but that the golden rule, which flows from moral equality, had to be lived.

As we will see in Chapter 5, in addition to the notion of equality, Christianity also introduced into Europe a commitment to reason and rational argument and the overall spirit of rational inquiry. It taught that because God acts rationally, there is an intelligible order governing the universe that we can understand. This insight led the Catholic Church, for example, to establish the first universities in the Middle Ages.

By introducing these ideas (equality, individual human dignity, and a spirit of rational inquiry) into European culture, Christianity was inadvertently sowing the seeds of a revolution that would ultimately undermine its influence and displace the Christian worldview from the dominant position that it held. Indeed, once the idea of the individual takes root, emphasizing his great dignity and equality, the individual will be tempted to reject the intellectual foundations of that idea, which he sees as constraining, and he will opt for an understanding of freedom as autonomy, as we see today in Expressive Individualism. And once the Church established the universities and instilled the notion of rational inquiry into European culture, it provided the individual with the intellectual tools he needed to contest the foundations of the Christian worldview.

The intellectual foundations of this revolution were laid by a number of thinkers over time, beginning as early as the 14th century. It is paradoxical that

1   Larry Sidentrop, *Inventing the Individual: The Origins of Western Liberalism* (Cambridge, Massachusetts: Belknap Press, 2014).

the vast majority of those who embrace Expressive Individualism today have never read the works of these thinkers and, in many cases, have never even heard of them. Nevertheless, their work represents a foundation and a precondition for the overthrow of the Christian worldview that accelerated in the last half of the 20th century. Without these ideas, Expressive Individualism could never have come about. We will now go on to briefly examine some of the most influential thinkers and movements whose theories have contributed to undermining the Christian worldview.

William of Ockham (1287-1347)

William of Ockham was an English Franciscan friar and philosopher, known for his development of nominalism, a philosophical position that holds that universals, or abstract concepts such as "justice" or "beauty," do not exist in reality but are merely names or labels that we apply to particular objects or individuals.

According to nominalism, only particular things or individuals exist in reality. For example, there is no universal concept of "dog," but only particular dogs that we classify as such. This is in opposition to moderate realism, which holds that universals have an independent existence that our minds are capable of grasping.

Nominalism consequently rejects the idea that man is able to know the nature of objects and so denies that man can attain true knowledge of reality, including God, through abstract reasoning. This position would exercise enormous influence on subsequent philosophers, such as Descartes, Kant, and others, who similarly deny that man can achieve genuine knowledge of the nature of objects. This was thus a first step on the long road to the Modern Self's embracing of empirical science as the only path to certain knowledge and its rejection of abstract reasoning as a way to prove the existence of God.[2]

Niccolò Machiavelli (1469-1527)

Niccolò Machiavelli was an Italian philosopher, diplomat, and political theorist. His political philosophy challenged the prevailing moral and ethical principles of his time that had been shaped by Christianity. Machiavelli wrote that the state should be governed by a strong and effective leader who was willing to use

---

2   Paul Spade and Claude Panaccio, "William of Ockham, no. 4.2 (The Rejection of Universals)," *Stanford Encyclopedia of Philosophy*, March 5, 2019, https://plato.stanford.edu/entries/ockham/index.html#ref-32.

any means necessary to maintain power and preserve the stability of the state. This included the use of violence, deception, and manipulation if necessary. He held that the end justifies the means and that the primary goal of the state is to ensure its survival and prosperity, even if this means sacrificing individual rights and freedoms.

This approach rejected the Christian Tradition's emphasis on virtue, piety, the common good, and the duty to govern according to the moral law. It also rejected Christianity's teaching to the effect that one may never do evil so that good may come of it. It represented another stage in the undermining of the Christian worldview. By contending that political leaders are not bound by natural law, it diminished the Church's ability to hold political leaders to account and laid the foundations for Expressive Individualism's wholesale rejection of natural law. Although his modern interpreters disagree about the extent to which Machiavelli really meant what he wrote to be taken seriously, it is undeniable that subsequent political philosophers, such as Hobbes, Rousseau, and Marx, accepted his thought at face value and were heavily influenced by him.[3]

The Protestant Reformation

The Protestant Reformation was a 16th century European religious reform movement that resulted in the creation of many religious groups (called Protestants) that separated from the Roman Catholic Church due to differences in doctrine. It rejected the traditional authority of the Catholic Church and emphasized the importance of individual conscience in matters of faith. Prior to the Reformation, the Catholic Church had been the central authority in matters of faith and religious doctrine. The Protestant Reformation rejected this authority and emphasized the importance of individual interpretation of scripture.

The Protestant Reformers were well intentioned, devout persons who sincerely believed that they were doing the work of God. However, as Brad S. Gregory has shown,[4] the Reformation had unintended consequences. Its emphasis on individual conscience and personal interpretation of scripture contributed to a rise in subjective morality and individualism, which emphasized the importance of personal autonomy, which is a hallmark of the Modern Self.

3   Cary Nederman, "Niccolò Machiavelli, no. 4 (Morality, Religion and Politics)," *Stanford Encyclopedia of Philosophy*, May 28, 2019, https://plato.stanford.edu/entries/machiavelli/#MoraReliPoli; George Sabine and Thomas Thorson, *A History of Political Theory, 4th Edition* (Orlando, Florida: Dryden Press, 1973), Chapter 18.

4   Brad Gregory, *The Unintended Reformation: How a Religious Revolution Secularized Society* (Cambridge, Massachusetts: Harvard University Press, 2012).

Gregory also points out that the Protestant Reformation led to a fragmentation of Christianity, ending the religious unity of Europe. It led to the loss of religious authority and hence to the loss of a shared moral and religious framework, all of which contributed to the eventual rise of the secularism espoused by Expressive Individualism today.

Rene Descartes (1596-1650)

The 17th century French philosopher Rene Descartes is often referred to as the Father of Modern Philosophy. It is paradoxical that he was a believing Catholic and saw his work as a contribution to Christian thought. Yet, although this was not his intention, he was the philosopher who started the trend of relativism and subjectivism that undermines the Christian worldview and has dominated philosophy since his time.

Descartes's contribution to subjectivism and relativism lies in two of his propositions. On the one hand, in order to arrive at certainty, at objective knowledge, he proposed to doubt everything that cannot be proven. This led him to conclude that the one truth that could not be doubted was the existence of himself as the doubting subject. In this way, he places thought, mental activity, at the very center of his philosophy. For Descartes, the only thing that we can know with certainty are our perceptions of things and not the things in themselves. Our own thought is the only unquestionable fact of our experience. Knowledge is the result of "innate ideas."

The second proposition that is key to the foundations of Expressive Individualism is the distinction that Descartes made between mind and body, referred to as Cartesian Dualism. And in making this distinction, Descartes gave priority to the mind. As we saw in Chapter One, Christianity teaches that, although man is indeed both corporeal and spiritual, in him spirit and matter are not two separate natures united, but rather their union forms a single human nature. The unity of soul and body is so profound that the soul is understood to be the form or animating principle of the body. It is the soul that makes the material body become a living, human body. By stressing the distinction of mind and body instead of their unity and by giving priority to the mind, Descartes prepared the way for modern Expressive Individualism, which also prioritizes one's inner psychological self and one's subjective experience over one's body and all external reality.

It is easy to see how Cartesian Dualism prepared the way for some particular manifestations of Expressive Individualism. For example, the transgender movement relies on the mind-body distinction when it affirms that the inner self can determine one's gender regardless of one's biological sex. In the same way, for the autonomous individual, since the unborn child has not yet developed a mind, it can't be considered a person. The same reasoning applies to people who are mentally disabled or suffer from dementia. If their minds no longer function properly and are unable to control their bodies, they have ceased to be full-fledged persons.

Philosophers after Descartes are often classified as either empiricists on the one hand or idealists and rationalists on the other. These differ as to what they believe is the source of knowledge. But they all agree in denying that we can know the essence or nature of a thing. Even empiricists, who hold that experience and observation of external reality are the proper source of knowledge, deny that we are able to grasp and know the nature of things. With Descartes, they contend that our perceptions of things are the proper object of knowledge and that we are unable to know things in themselves.[5]

Thomas Hobbes (1588-1679)

Hobbes, who was an important 17th century British political philosopher, upheld a theory known as the Social Contract. This is the view that our rights and obligations are a result of a social contract or agreement and do not belong to us by virtue of our human nature or our human dignity.

Hobbes is famous for his thought experiment concerning the state of nature. He says that in a world without any political institutions, people would be constantly fighting amongst themselves out of a desire for personal gain (or preserving what they already have). In other words, he says that a state of nature is a state of war. Because early humans did not enjoy living under such conditions, they proposed a social contract outlining laws and obligations that are conducive to peace and elected a sovereign to enforce such a contract.

According to social contract theory, all human rights and obligations are socially constructed. Prior to the establishment of the basic social contract, nothing is immoral or unjust—anything goes. After these contracts are established, however, society becomes possible, and people can be expected to keep their promises, cooperate with one another, and so on. The Social Contract is the most fundamental source of all that is good and that which we depend upon to live well. Our choice is either to abide by the terms of the contract or return to the State of Nature, which Hobbes argues no reasonable person could possibly prefer. Social contract theory is opposed to the traditional Christian understanding of man as a child of God, possessing an inherent dignity and

---

5   Lex Newman, "Descartes' Epistemology, no. 4.1 (Cogito Ergo Sum)," *Stanford Encyclopedia of Philosophy*, February 15, 2019, https://plato.stanford.edu/entries/descartes-epistemology/#CogiErgoSum; Howard Robinson, "Dualism, no. 1.2 (History of Dualism)," *Stanford Encyclopedia of Philosophy*, September 11, 2020, https://plato.stanford.edu/entries/dualism/.

rights that should not be violated. It leads to the moral relativism of the Autonomous Individual, which states that all morality is socially constructed and subject to change and denies that there exist universal, absolute, and objective moral norms.[6]

John Locke (1632-1704)

John Locke was an influential 17th century English philosopher. He is often referred to as the "father of liberalism" due to his development of many key principles that have shaped modern democratic societies. Like Hobbes, Locke was also a social contract theorist, which means that his political philosophy had a similar effect on the decline of Christian thought in western civilization. It was, however, in his writings on human knowledge that his influence on the development of Expressive Individualism is most apparent. Scholastic philosophers had held that the main goal of metaphysics and science was to learn about the real essence of things: the key metaphysical components of things that explain all their interesting features. It is what Scholastics referred to as the substantial form of a being. Locke thought this project was misguided. He believed that the real essence of beings is entirely unknown and undiscoverable by us. This led him to suggest an alternative way to understand and investigate nature. He recommends focusing on what he refers to as the nominal essences of things.

For Locke, nominal essences are indeed knowable and are the best way to understand individual substances. Nominal essences are just collections of all the observed features an individual thing possesses. So, the nominal essence of a piece of gold would include the ideas of yellowness, a certain weight, malleability, dissolvability in certain chemicals, and so on.

Locke offers us an analogy to illustrate the difference between real and nominal essences. He suggests that our position with respect to ordinary objects is like the position of someone looking at a very complicated clock. The gears, wheels, weights, and pendulum that produce the motions of the hands on the clock face (the clock's real essence) are unknown to the person. They are hidden behind the casing. He or she can only know about the observable features like the clock's shape, the movement of the hands, and the chiming of the hours (the clock's nominal essence). Similarly, when we look at an object like a dandelion, we are only able to observe its nominal essence (the yellow color, the bitter smell, and so forth). We have no clear idea what produces these features of the dandelion or how they are produced.

---

6   Sharon Lloyd and Susanne Sreedhar, "Hobbes' Moral and Political Philosophy," *Stanford Encyclopedia of Philosophy*, September 12, 2020, https://plato.stanford.edu/entries/hobbes-moral/.

Locke's metaphysical skepticism is important because it denies that we can acquire any objective knowledge about the real essence of things, and so denies that we can have any true knowledge about the existence of God and his qualities and about man and the world. Without this knowledge, we can't acquire a true grasp of human nature and are so unable to know the natural law and establish a basis for ethics. It leads directly to the skepticism that we see in Expressive Individualism, which denies that we can know that there is such a thing as human nature and holds that there is no universal absolute and objective natural law.[7]

David Hume (1711-1776)

David Hume was influential in developing the empiricist school of philosophy, which remains popular to this day. Empiricism is the view that all knowledge is derived fundamentally from experience and nothing else. This position is typically contrasted with the rationalist view to the effect that knowledge can be derived from experience as well as from reason alone. How does empiricism undermine the Christian worldview? Empiricism erodes belief in God because, for an empiricist, knowledge of the existence of God must rest fundamentally on experience. A priori proofs for the existence of God using reason (e.g., ontological or cosmological arguments) do not amount to genuine knowledge, according to an empiricist.

So, we can see that Hume exercised an important influence on Expressive Individualism. As we saw in Chapter 2, for the Modern Self, the empirical method is considered the only way to obtain reliable knowledge, and any knowledge obtained via a method that deviates from this approach is seen as less certain and somehow flawed. And since Christian theology and ethics cannot be verified by a scientific test, they are not considered real knowledge and so are not worthy of belief.

Hume is also known for his critique of moral realism, the position that there are objective moral truths. Instead, Hume's ethical theory is a kind of moral sentimentalism (sometimes referred to as emotivism): the view that moral judgements are nothing more than expressions of emotions or sentiments. To give an example, suppose one considers that abortion is wrong. According to Hume's sentimentalism, this judgement is akin to an expression of emotion like "down with abortion!" indicating that we have negative feelings as regards the practice. However, expressions of emotions have no truth value. "1+1=2" is either true or false; "the human body is approximately 70% water" is true or

---

7   Jan-Erik Jones, "Locke on Real Essence," *Stanford Encyclopedia of Philosophy*, September 22, 2022, https://plato.stanford.edu/entries/real-essence/#ReaEssSub.

false; but "down with abortion!" is not the kind of sentence that can be true or false, in the same way that "Hooray Raptors!" cannot have any truth value. In Hume's ethical theory, all moral judgements are of this sort and thus are neither true nor false. That is to say, there is no objective morality. We can consequently see that Hume had a major influence on Expressive Individualism, which embraces his moral sentimentalism and denies that there can be any universal, absolute, and objective moral norms.

Finally, Hume is also significant for his attacks on religious belief, his argument against belief in miracles being one of the most significant. In Section X of his Enquiry Concerning Human Understanding, Hume tells us that it is not reasonable to subscribe to any "system of religion" unless that system is validated by the occurrence of miracles. He then argues that we cannot be justified in believing that a miracle has occurred, at least when our belief is based on testimony—as when, for example, it is based on the reports of miracles that are given in scripture. A miracle is, according to Hume, a violation of a physical law. We suppose that a physical law obtains only when we have an extensive, and exceptionless, experience of a certain kind of phenomenon. For example, we suppose that, according to physical laws, a human being cannot walk on the surface of water while it is in its liquid state. This supposition is based on the weight of an enormous body of experience gained from our familiarity with what happens in seas, lakes, kitchen sinks, and bathtubs. Given that experience, we always have the best possible evidence that in any particular case, an object with a sufficiently great average density, having been placed onto the surface of a body of water, will sink. According to Hume, the evidence in favour of a miracle, even when that is provided by the strongest possible testimony, will always be outweighed by the evidence for the physical law, which is supposed to have been violated. Once again, we see that Expressive Individualism has adopted Hume's critique, denying the possibility of miracles and, by extension, denying the truth of sacred scripture and hence rejecting the entire Christian Faith.[8]

Jean-Jacques Rousseau (1712–1778)

Jean-Jacques Rousseau was an influential 18th century thinker from Geneva. As Carl Trueman has stated, his significance for the history of Expressive Individualism lies in the fact that Rousseau

> offers a compelling and influential articulation of two ideas that help us
> understand the modern notion of the self. First, he locates identity in

---

8   William Morris and Charlotte Brown, "David Hume, no. 3 (Philosophical Project)," *Stanford Encyclopedia of Philosophy*, April 17, 2019, https://plato.stanford.edu/entries/ hume/#PhiPro.

the inner psychological life of the individual. Feelings for Rousseau are central to who we are. And second, he sees society (or perhaps better, culture) as exerting a corrupting influence on the self. To the extent that society prevents us from acting consistently with our feelings, to that extent it prevents us from being who we really are. In short, society makes us inauthentic.[9]

Up until the time of Rousseau, it was understood that one's identity was bound up with one's place in society and in one's family. Everyone experienced emotions and feelings, of course. But their expression was dictated and limited by one's position. The virtue of self-restraint was of paramount importance. Rousseau undermines this way of thinking, maintaining that identity is to be found in the inner psychological life of the individual and that in order to be free, everyone should be authentic by giving expression to their feelings and emotions.

Rousseau understood man to be born free, pristine, and innocent. Whereas Christianity teaches that we are born subject to original sin and concupiscence (a tendency to seek satisfaction in base pleasures and selfishness), Rousseau believes that it is society and culture that introduce wickedness into our lives and corrupt and pervert the individual. Society, civilization, obliges us to act with hypocrisy, forcing us to follow norms and conventions that are unnatural to us and prevent us from being who we truly are, from acting according to that inner, uncorrupted voice of our nature. If we were left in the state of nature, instead of being ruled by artificial social institutions, we would be able to act with freedom and be who we truly are. This vision of Rousseau, which bases sentiment at the heart of ethics and gives priority to personal preference, articulates the modern notion of the self that prevails in Western society today.

How did it happen that Rousseau's notions about feelings and the inner, psychological life came to dominate the worldview of the Modern Self? According to Trueman, the answer lies in the 19th century Romantic movement, above all in three of the great poets of that movement: William Wordsworth, Percy Shelley, and William Blake. Without their influence, Rousseau's ideas would probably have remained at the level of theoretical debate among intellectuals and have never penetrated deeply into the culture. It was Shelley who referred to the poet and poetry as the "midwife," the one who, through his passion and art, gives life to and transmits this new vision of the self. As with Rousseau, for these Romantic poets, priority is to be granted to feelings and instincts, which should form the basis of moral action. They are the true guides to who we really are:

> ...the Romantics grant an authority to feelings, to that inner psychological space, that all humans possess. And those feelings are

9   Carl Trueman, *Strange New World* (Wheaton, Illinois: Crossway, 2022), 34-35.

first and foremost genuine, pristine and true guides to who human beings are. It is only society, with its petty rivalries, its competitiveness and its artificial sophistication, that twists, perverts and distorts those feelings. This is a key move in the path to the modern self, made more compelling by the fact that it is expressed in an artistic form rather than a philosophical argument.[10]

Of course, it is obvious that when one considers feelings as the foundation for ethics, then taste and simple personal preference become the decisive factors in determining what is good and evil. When taste and personal preference are detached from any universal and authoritative notion of morality and of what it means to be human, then feelings rule. Indeed, in such a case, feelings become truth. This is why Rousseau, Wordsworth, Blake, and Shelley made use of poetry to achieve the moral reformation of individuals and of society. Their poetry gives expression to Rousseau's psychological man, and this thread makes its way from the Romantic period into the present. Trueman refers to these poets as the "Unacknowledged Legislators." Their works were like fuel poured on a smouldering fire. Their poetry, which was extremely popular, imbedded this expressivism into the culture of 19th century Europe.

Immanuel Kant (1724-1804)

Immanuel Kant is the central figure in modern philosophy. He synthesized early modern rationalism and empiricism, set the terms for much of 19th and 20th century philosophy, and continues to exercise a significant influence today in all areas of philosophy. One of Kant's major projects is to reach a "decision about the possibility or impossibility of a metaphysics in general." He begins his metaphysical project with the premise that human beings experience only appearances, not things in themselves. Thus, there is a fundamental divide between our sensory perceptions and the world itself, between a world of appearances and another world of things in themselves.

For Kant, things in themselves are absolutely real in the sense that they would exist and have whatever properties they have even if no human beings were around to perceive them. Appearances, on the other hand, are not absolutely real because their existence and properties depend on human perceivers. Moreover, whenever appearances do exist, in some sense they exist in the minds of human perceivers. So, appearances are mental entities or mental representations. All our experiences, all our perceptions of objects and events, fall into the class of appearances that exist in the minds of human perceivers.

10 Trueman, *Strange New World*, 46.

Kant's metaphysics leads to a kind of radical skepticism that traps each of us within the contents of our own mind and cuts us off from reality. We can see how Kant's theory feeds directly into the mindset of the autonomous individual, who contends that that our interior, psychological life and beliefs must be given priority, to which external reality must conform.

Kant's moral philosophy also takes a subjective turn. Instead of placing the source of morality in the purpose for which we were created and our human nature, he holds that the moral law arises from our subjective capacity for autonomy. For Kant, we are autonomous in the sense that we are able to rationally choose our own courses of action; we have the capacity to act against our immediate desires or urges. Since all humans possess reason (and are thus free), the actions that reason demands must be universalizable across human beings. Thus, Kant says that we should "act according to the maxim that you would wish all other rational people to follow, as if it were a universal law." Therefore, for Kant, the entirety of the moral law is sourced from our autonomy.

Kant was a profound thinker, and his ethical theory is quite nuanced. Expressive Individualism has adopted Kant's teaching that the source of morality lies in our autonomy but has adopted it in a simplistic way without fully understanding the meaning that Kant ascribed to the notion of autonomy. Kant thus inadvertently made a significant contribution to the development of today's Expressive Individualism in spite of his intentions to the contrary.[11]

John Stuart Mill (1806-1873)

John Stuart Mill was a British political philosopher, political economist, and one of the most influential thinkers in the history of classical liberalism. Mill is best known for his development in ethics and political philosophy. In ethics he is known for his utilitarianism. Roughly, this is the view that the morally right action is the one that results in the greatest amount of net happiness for everyone. To give an example, suppose one sees a drowning child and decides to save him. What is it that makes this action right? A deontologist like Kant might say that saving the child was the only action that could be willed to be a universal moral law, hence it was right. A virtue ethicist like Aristotle might say that saving the child was the virtuous thing to do, hence it was right. A Christian would contend that we are called to love everyone and that saving the child is a way to express one's love for the child. Mill, a utilitarian, would instead say that saving

---

11   Michelle Grier, "Kant's Critique of Metaphysics," *Stanford Encyclopedia of Philosophy*, September 14, 2022, https://plato.stanford.edu/entries/kant-metaphysics/; Robert Johnson and Adam Cureton "Kant's Moral Philosophy no. 10 (Autonomy)," *Stanford Encyclopedia of Philosophy*, January 21, 2022, https://plato.stanford.edu/entries/kant-moral/.

the child was right because, had you not done it, there would be less happiness in the world. It is immediately obvious that utilitarianism is incompatible with the Christian worldview. For example, according to this principle it would be justifiable to kill two innocent people in order to save three, since there would be more happiness in the world if one simply killed the two. However, for a Christian it is never permissible to take an innocent human life for any reason whatsoever. Utilitarianism also leads to Expressive Individualism. As we saw in Chapter 2, for the autonomous individual, happiness lies in being true to one's inner self and in exercising one's autonomy by engaging in activities that produce psychological well being. For Expressive individualism, then, we should always act in a way that allows the greatest number of people to exercise their autonomy, since that produces the greatest amount of happiness.

In political philosophy, Mill is well known as the thinker who first popularized the Harm principle. This is the doctrine that "the only purpose for which power can be rightfully exercised over any member of a civilized community, against his will, is to prevent harm to others."[12] For Mill, the priority must be to allow each person to exercise his autonomy, so long as he does not harm others. As he stated,

> the only freedom which deserves the name, is that of pursuing our own good in our own way, so long as we do not attempt to deprive others of theirs, or impede their efforts to obtain it. Each is the proper guardian of his own health, whether bodily, or mental and spiritual. Mankind are greater gainers by suffering each other to live as seems good to themselves, than by compelling each to live as seems good to the rest.[13]

As we saw in Chapter 2, this doctrine (the Do No Harm principle) has been entirely adopted by Expressive Individualism and has even become one of its leitmotifs. It is opposed to Christian moral teaching since it fails to concern itself with notions of virtue, justice, natural law, etc.[14]

Charles Darwin (1809-1882)

Darwin was an English naturalist and biologist best known for his theory of evolution by natural selection, which holds that species change and adapt

---

12   John Mill, "Chapter I. Introductory" in *On Liberty* (London: John W. Parker and Son, 1859), 22, *Project Gutenberg*, https://www.gutenberg.org/cache/epub/34901/pg34901-images.html.

13   Mill, *On Liberty*, 13

14   Christopher Macleod, "John Stuart Mill," *Stanford Encyclopedia of Philosophy*, August 25, 2016, https://plato.stanford.edu/entries/mill/; Sabine and Thorson, *A History of Political Theory, 4th Edition*, 638-646.

over time. This theory greatly influenced the development of philosophical naturalism, which holds that all that exists belongs to the natural world without reference to supernatural entities or agencies. It contends that nature is the order of things accessible to us through observation and the methods of the empirical sciences. Darwin was so instrumental in the rise of naturalism because, for the first time in history, many phenomena that previously seemed to require supernatural explanations could now be explained naturally through evolution.

Naturalism denies that there is any distinctively metaphysical area of inquiry. It is a conception of reality as homogeneous in the sense that there is one natural order that comprises all of reality. There are no objects or properties that can only be identified or comprehended by metaphysical theorizing or non-empirical understanding. If some other method, such as a priori theorizing, is needed to have access to an alleged entity or to truth, then it is not a real entity or a genuine truth. As we saw in Chapter 2, this philosophical naturalism has been adopted by Expressive Individualism.

Darwin's theory of evolution by natural selection seemed to challenge some key tenets of the Christian worldview and, therefore, undermine the religious beliefs of many people. For example, proposing that species evolve over time through natural selection rather than being created in their current form by a divine being contradicted the literalist interpretation of the Bible, which holds that God created all living things in their present form over the course of six days. Of course, the Church had never taught a literalist interpretation of Biblical chronology, but many people believed in it. In addition, Darwin's theory undermined the Christian worldview by implying that humans are not the special creation of God but rather evolved from earlier, simpler forms of life. This challenged the Christian teaching to the effect that humans are the summit of creation and possess a unique place in the universe. Once again, Expressive Individualism has embraced this naturalist explanation, denying any special status to humans.[15]

Karl Marx (1818-1883)

Karl Marx was a German political theorist and socialist revolutionary. His main influence on Expressive Individualism has been his theory of class struggle, which he believed to be the main driving force of historical change. Marx saw this struggle as being mainly about economic issues (control of the means of production and the distribution of wealth and resources). In his theory of

---

15   Phillip Sloan, "Darwin: From Origin of Species to Descent of Man," *Stanford Encyclopedia of Philosophy*, June 17, 2019, https://plato.stanford.edu/entries/origin-descent/.

history, in all epochs there has been a constant tension between the oppressors (victimizers) and the oppressed (victims).

The Neo-Marxist Frankfurt School, including thinkers like Herbert Marcuse, Theodor Adorno, Erich Fromm, and Max Horkheimer, shifted the emphasis from economic injustice to a critique based more on cultural and sociological inequities. They maintained that society's norms and institutions were suppressing individuality and emphasized the importance of authenticity and self-realization. Their ideas significantly influenced the countercultural movements of the 1960s and 1970s, which championed personal freedom, self-expression, and opposition to mainstream cultural norms. Their influence can be seen in the Black Lives Matter movement, the LGBQ+ movement, radical feminism, Critical Race Theory, the Social Justice crusade, etc. These are all based on the Marxist notion of the struggle between oppressors and victims. What they hold in common is the assumption that any individual can fulfill himself by socially and sometimes violently opposing whatever frustrates his personal preferences or desires.[16]

Friedrich Nietzsche (1844-1900)

Friedrich Nietzsche was a 19th century German philosopher. One of his major influences on the development of philosophy is his nihilism—the view that no objective values such as good, evil, or meaning exist in the world. He maintains that all value is simply a result of social construction. For example, humans might say that murder is wrong or that temperance is good, but independent of the human mind, these moral concepts are simply non-existent. In reality, there is no such thing as the good, for instance. To illustrate this point, Nietzsche claims: "Whatever has value in our world now does not have value in itself, according to its nature (nature is always valueless), but has been given value at some time, as a present, and it was we who gave and bestowed it."[17]

Even though Nietzsche does not believe in the objectivity of value, he nonetheless recommends some ideals that we should live by (though he acknowledges that these are not values in any objective sense). One of Nietzsche's core values is the will to power. A well-known passage appears near the opening of the late work, The Antichrist: "What is good? Everything that heightens the feeling of power in man, the will to power, power itself. What is bad? Everything that is born of weakness. What is happiness? The feeling that power is growing,

16 Sabine and Thorson, *A History of Political Theory*, chapter 34..
17 Nietzsche, Friedrich (1882), *The Gay Science*, trans. W. Kaufmann (New York: Vintage, 1974), 301.

that resistance is overcome."[18] Nietzsche thinks first that all human beings are naturally attracted to enhancing their own power. And secondly, because this desire for power constitutes our nature, he thinks that, normatively, it is good to develop these natural capacities. In other words, a good life consists in acquiring and enhancing our own power.

Nietzsche's philosophy thus emphasizes individual autonomy and self-expression. It upholds the importance of the individual and the rejection of traditional values and morality. He contends that individuals should be free to create their own values and pursue their own goals without being inhibited by socially accepted norms or moral principles. As is obvious, this emphasis on individual freedom and autonomy greatly contributed to the development of Expressive Individualism which has completely adopted Nietzsche's position. In addition, Nietzsche rejected the concept of objective truth and argued that the self is constantly evolving, which has contributed to Expressive Individualism's stance on identity and self-realization.[19]

Sigmund Freud (1856-1939)

Sigmund Freud was an Austrian neurologist and the founder of psychoanalysis. His work undermined the Christian worldview and influenced the development of Expressive Individualism in several ways. Freud denied the existence of the human soul, contending that the mind is merely the product of the brain. This laid the groundwork for Expressive Individualism's rejection of the Christian belief in the afterlife and the concept of the soul's immortality. Freud also held that religion is an illusion created by human beings to cope with their unconscious fears and desires, rather than divinely revealed truth. Once again, this notion has been taken up by Expressive Individualism.

Freud developed the idea of the unconscious mind, which emphasizes the role of individual desires and experiences that are not necessarily rational or conscious. This contributed to the rise of the Modern Self by focusing on the uniqueness and inner world of each person. It showed that individuals have a complex inner life that shapes their identities and actions. It gave importance to subjective experiences, personal desires, dreams, and aspirations and emphasized self-exploration and self-understanding. He encouraged individuals to gain insight into their own motivations, conflicts, and desires. This process of self-reflection and self-discovery encouraged individuals to understand and assert their own individuality, separate from society's expectations and norms.

18 Nietzsche, Friedrich. [1895] 1924, The Antichrist (2nd ed.), translated by H. L. Mencken (New York: Alfred A. Knopf., 1918), Section 2.

19 R. Anderson, "Friedrich Nietzsche," Stanford Encyclopedia of Philosophy, May 19, 2022, https://plato.stanford.edu/entries/nietzsche/.

Freud laid great emphasis on the importance of childhood experiences in shaping adult behavior. His focus on one's unique personal history and experiences challenged traditional notions of fixed social roles and identities, laying the groundwork for Expressive Individualism's embracing of identity as something malleable.

His theory of psychosexual development rejected the sexual self-restraint advocated by traditional and religious norms, and emphasized the importance of sexual freedom and of exploring and understanding one's own sexual desires and experiences. By doing away with traditional sexual taboos, Freud paved the way for the sexual revolution which is the supreme accomplishment of Expressive Individualism.[20]

The Rise of Expressive individualism in the 20th Century

It was in the latter half of the 20th century that Expressive Individualism in fact displaced Christianity as the dominant worldview in the West. The groundwork had been laid over a period of 600 years by the thinkers we have mentioned. But beginning in the early 1960s, there was a rapid acceleration in the rise of Expressive Individualism in the culture and mindset of the general population. This can be attributed to several key movements that championed ideas emphasizing personal freedom, self-expression, and the pursuit of individual desires. Below we set out some of the more important of these movements.

The Sexual Revolution

The sexual revolution, which has been embraced by Expressive Individualism, was a social and cultural movement of the 20th Century whose ultimate goal was the elimination of all sexual taboos. It challenged traditional norms and attitudes towards sexuality, advocated for sexual liberation, and paved the way for greater acceptance and understanding of different sexual orientations and relationships. Most importantly, and thanks in large part to the marketing of the contraceptive pill, it legitimized the separation between the unitive and procreative dimensions of sexual intercourse, thus opening the way to what came to be understood as "recreational sex." No one person or group of persons effected the revolution.[21] Nevertheless, there were several influential figures and

---

20   John Hill, *After the Natural Law* (San Francisco: Ignatius Press, 2016), 170-174.

21   For an insightful study of this topic, see, Alan Petigny, *The Permissive Society in America, 1941-1965*, (Cambridge: Cambridge University Press, 2009).

movements that played important roles in its emergence, among whom were the following:

Alfred Kinsey was an American sexologist who carried out pioneering research on human sexuality in the 1940s and 1950s. His studies set out the diversity and complexity of sexual behavior, thereby challenging prevailing notions of sexuality. They contributed to the destigmatization of discussions about sexuality and established the foundation for more open attitudes. It is true that his research has subsequently been shown to have been deeply flawed. But it nevertheless had a major influence on Western views regarding sexuality.[22]

Wilhelm Reich was an Austrian psychoanalyst, and psychiatrist who promoted sexual liberation and the inclusion of sexual health into psychoanalysis. He held that sexual repression was a source of psychological disorders and emphasized the importance of sexual fulfillment for psychological well-being. Reich's ideas played a significant role in shaping the wider conversation on sexual liberation.[23]

Margaret Sanger was an American birth control activist and founder of the American Birth Control League, which later became Planned Parenthood. She campaigned for women's reproductive rights, access to contraception, and family planning. Sanger's advocacy contributed to the sexual revolution by challenging traditional taboos regarding contraception and promoting sexual autonomy.[24]

Hugh Hefner, the founder of Playboy magazine, played a role in the popularization and commercialization of sexual freedom. Playboy, launched in 1953, featured articles on sexual topics as well as nude photography. Hefner's work challenged conservative attitudes towards sexuality and promoted a more emancipated and liberated approach.[25]

The Feminist Movement, particularly the second wave feminism of the 1960s and 1970s, was a crucial force in the sexual revolution. Feminists championed women's reproductive rights, sexual autonomy, and an end to sexual double standards. They opposed traditional constraints that limited women's sexual freedom and thus played a significant role in transforming societal attitudes towards sexuality.[26]

The LGBTQ+ Movement advocated for LGBTQ+ rights and played a significant role in the sexual revolution. The Stonewall Riots of 1969, led

---

22   Alan Branch, "The Godfather of Gay Rights," Mercatornet, December 2, 2015, https://web.archive.org/web/20230201231000/https://www.mercatornet.com/godfather-of-gay-rights/19898/.

23   Carl Trueman, *The Rise and Triumph of the Modern Self* (Wheaton, Illinois: Crossway, 2020), 232-244.

24   Jonah Goldberg, *Liberal Fascism* (New York, New York: Doubleday, 2008), 270-274.

25   Trueman, *The Rise and Triumph of the Modern Self*, 280-285.

26   Trueman, *The Rise and Triumph of the Modern Self*, 254-263.

by some LGBTQ+ individuals, marked a turning point in the gay rights movement and sparked increased visibility and activism. The LGBTQ+ movement promoted sexual freedom, the decriminalization of homosexuality, and recognition of a wide range of sexual orientations and gender identities. The transgender movement, in particular, expanded society's understanding of gender beyond the traditional binary concept of male and female and rejected the notion that gender is solely determined by biological sex. The movement's success was largely based on the general acceptance that the unitive and procreative aspects of sexuality could be understood as separable and that sex could thus be seen as something essentially recreational and only optionally procreative.

The Beat Generation Writers

The Beat Generation writers of the 1950s and 1960s, including figures like Jack Kerouac, Allen Ginsberg, and William S. Burroughs, rebelled against social conformity and advocated for personal freedom and self-expression. Through their literature and poetry, they expressed a rejection of traditional norms and a celebration of individualism and countercultural values. Their work inspired a generation of artists, musicians, and writers who sought to challenge established structures and embrace alternative lifestyles. They tackled taboo subjects, including sexuality and drug use, in a way that challenged the prevailing Christian outlook. They were instrumental in inspiring such subsequent movements as feminism and LGBTQ+ rights, as their work gave voice to marginalized groups and advocated for social justice. They thus sowed many ideas that were subsequently taken up by Expressive Individualism. Furthermore, a good number of those who were affected by these ideas obtained posts as university professors and used their positions to sow Expressive Individualism in the universities.[27]

Existentialism

Existentialist philosophy was rampant on university campuses in the 1960s and 1970s. Existentialist philosophers like Jean-Paul Sartre, Albert Camus, and Simone de Beauvoir emphasized individual freedom, personal authenticity, subjective experience, and self-definition. Existentialism contended that life

---

27   For a fuller description of the influence of the Beat Generation writers, cf. William Manchester, *The Glory and the Dream, A Narrative History of America, 1932-1972* (Boston, Mass.: Little Brown 1973) 726-729

is absurd and meaningless and encouraged individuals to take responsibility for exploring their authentic selves and creating their own values, meaning, and purpose. It contributed to the rise of the autonomous individual by providing a philosophical framework that validated and supported the idea of personal freedom and self-expression while undermining traditional notions of identity, morality, and societal expectations, paving the way for a more individualistic worldview.[28]

The Entertainment Industry

Movies, music, television, and other forms of entertainment have made a significant contribution to the rise of expressive individualism and continue to promote that worldview. They frequently explore themes of personal freedom, self-discovery, and the pursuit of individual passions. In films, the characters often represent countercultural values and rebellion against authority. In this way, they popularize the idea that individuals have the right to express themselves freely and pursue their own unique paths. They also often explore issues of race, gender, sexuality, and identity, thereby promoting inclusivity, equality, and diversity, challenging traditional social hierarchies, fostering the normalization and acceptance of these lifestyles, and promoting the idea that there are many valid paths to personal fulfillment. Furthermore, celebrities and popular figures in the entertainment world often become icons. Since the vast majority of them have embraced Expressive Individualism, they essentially become spokespersons for that worldview and influence their millions of fans to embrace it as well.

Internet, Social Media and Digital Platforms

The advent of the internet and of social media and digital platforms has further amplified the spread of Expressive Individualism in popular culture. Platforms like Instagram, YouTube, and TikTok have empowered individuals to share their unique perspectives, talents, and stories directly with a global audience. This democratization of content creation has enabled individuals to express themselves authentically and connect with like-minded individuals, fostering a sense of community and solidarity. Finally, it has popularized the concept of personal branding and self-presentation, encouraging individuals to carefully curate and showcase their unique

---

28 Kevin Aho, "Existentialism," *Stanford Encyclopedia of Philosophy*, January 6, 2023, https://plato.stanford.edu/entries/existentialism/.

personas to the world. This focus on self-presentation has contributed to the rise of Expressive Individualism by emphasizing the importance of individual identity and personal style. The over-indulgence of young people in social media communication, coupled with screen addiction, tends to overwhelm the reasoning powers of many young people as well as older people with immature instincts who are conditioned by social media. They simply cannot consider things dispassionately, nor do the social media platforms want them to. They are unable to mount a serious critique of the worldview of Expressive Individualism.

Consumer Culture and the Mass Media

The rise of consumer culture in the 20th century has also contributed to the rapid spread of Expressive Individualism. It portrays consumption as a means of empowerment and self-expression. Through advertising and marketing strategies, individuals are encouraged to associate certain products or experiences with specific personal attributes or values. This has created a culture where consumption is seen as a way to express individuality, communicate one's identity, and differentiate oneself from others.

Movements in Favour of Progressive Education

Several educational theories and perspectives that gained prominence over the latter half of the 20th century led to a de-emphasis on the teaching of Western Civilization. These included Postcolonial Theory, Multiculturalism, Critical Theory, the Social Justice Movement, etc.

The consequent removal of courses in philosophy as well as theology in public and private universities starting in the 1950s and the general discrediting of the teaching of Western Civilization left people without any reasonable understanding of their life and history. Without a strong emphasis on cultural heritage, traditions, and historical narratives in education, individuals struggle to develop a coherent sense of identity and belonging. Education historically provided a framework through which people could connect to their cultural roots and understand their place within a larger societal context. This lack of rootedness and sense of identity leaves people more susceptible to the influence of the mass media, the main message of which is Expressive Individualism.

Unsurprisingly, all these contributors and movements were interconnected and influenced one another. They collectively contributed to the shifting cultural and philosophical landscape, promoting the ideals of personal autonomy, self-expression, and the pursuit of individual desires that characterize expressive individualism in the 21st century.

This completes our brief study of how Expressive Individualism displaced Christianity as the dominant worldview in the West in the latter half of the 20th century. In the next chapter, we will examine Expressive Individualism's position on Natural Law and a philosophical refutation of that position.

Chapter 4

The Case for Natural Law

It is clear that Expressive Individualism is incompatible with the Christian worldview. If a Christian wishes to challenge Expressive Individualism, how is he to proceed? He cannot use the Scriptures, since the Expressive Individualist does not accept that they are divinely inspired. Therefore, the Christian can only have recourse to arguments from reason. His first step is to make the case for natural law, since much of Expressive Individualism is predicated on a denial of natural law.

As we saw in Chapter 1, the Christian tradition holds that the natural moral law (also called the natural law or the moral law) is written on the heart of each man. It is an objective standard for what is morally right or wrong, which human beings can know, at least in its basic principles. This standard applies to all human beings. The natural moral law is not a law imposed on man from outside. It is not top-down in any sense. The moral principles that constitute the natural moral law are based on and flow from man's nature. Given that nature, they are the principles that he needs to follow in order to become all that he is meant to be, and lead a happy and meaningful life.

In Expressive Individualism the world is essentially a product of chance. We are not naturally subject to any laws other than the laws of physics. Each man is considered the origin and cause of his own moral law. A man does not discover an objective moral law that already exists. He creates his own, deciding by what moral rules he will live. Expressive Individualism thus embraces moral relativism. Yet, even though for the Expressive Individualist there is no natural law, in order to live together in peace and harmony, humans have adopted the Golden Rule and the Do No Harm Principle. Without these, society would descend into chaos. But these principles are strictly utilitarian: they are necessary for social peace. They do not flow necessarily from our nature. In fact, as we saw in Chapter 2, many Expressive Individualists deny that there is such a thing as a fixed human nature shared by all men and women. It is rather considered to be something very malleable. This malleability is deemed necessary in order to construct one's identity. Expressive Individualists would say

> I have no given nature; I am my own life-project; I make myself. My project, both in its formulation and in its realization, is determined by nothing else than what I choose. There is no such thing as a nature

> within which I must work, or a truth that rules me from above. I am free
> to make my own nature, my own truth, and my own values.[1]

Natural law, on the other hand, takes human nature as its starting point. So the first point is to show that a fixed human nature does exist and then to go on to show that there is indeed a natural moral law. So, what do we mean by nature?

All living beings tend to grow and mature until they reach their full development; this is their "end," or telos. All living beings are perfected when they fulfill their natural function. This is what is "good" for them. By the term "good," we mean what is fitting and proper for the being, not morally good. And what is good for the being has the character of an end or goal. For example, the good or end of an eagle is to soar, hunt, and mate. If the eagle is kept locked up alone in a small cage, instead of flourishing, it will deteriorate, sicken, and die. These tendencies in living beings are intrinsic and innate, rooted in the beings themselves and not imposed from the outside. The source or root of these inclinations is what we call their nature. This nature is not some abstract being of reason. It is the essence of a being understood as the principle of operations of that kind of being.

The Notion of Human Nature

Since a person is a living human being, then we can say that, like all living beings, he has a principle of operations that leads him to reach his telos, or "end." This is what we call human nature: that condition in man that makes it possible for him to develop towards his full potential and reach his fulfillment. This human nature is largely responsible for a person's dynamism. Man naturally seeks to acquire knowledge, skills, material goods, relationships, etc. because his human nature leads him to perceive that these are necessary for life, culture, acceptance, friends, etc. If there were no such thing as "human nature," if human beings had nothing in common, then the term "humanity" would mean nothing. Expressive Individualism firmly contends all persons are equal, that each person has human rights, and that the defense of these rights is the safeguard of a just and democratic society. But if one refuses to recognize the existence of a universal human nature, on what grounds can one defend the notion of equality and human rights (i.e., rights that we possess by the mere fact of being human) since the term being human would have no meaning? We can speak about persons, or human beings precisely because we recognize that, even though each one is very different, each one has some essential characteristics

---

1   Cormac Burke, *Man and Values - A Personalist Anthropology* (Strongsville: Scepter Publishers, 2008), 213.

in common with all other men: an intellect and free will, a conscience, basic human rights, etc.

A person can forge his own character, his own identity. He can choose his own values and is able to lead the kind of life he chooses, to pursue the goals that he prefers. But this does not mean that human nature is transient and ephemeral, varying from person to person and changing as historical and cultural situations change. If human nature is what a person shares with all other people, then it must be independent of personal, cultural, and historical factors.

Anthropology is the social science that studies humans, human behavior and human society past and present. Anthropologists conclude that all men and women, across history and across cultures, are subject to and experience the same passions: love and hatred, desire and fear, joy, sadness, and anger. They all seek happiness. They are naturally self-centered. They all find it difficult to live self-discipline, order, generosity, etc. All of this shows clearly that we are all subject to the same human nature. Thus, the Expressive Individualist denial of human nature is untenable. It has taken the fact that we are able to choose our own values and forge our own identity and erroneously understood this to mean that we have no common human nature.

As we just saw, human nature "imposes" certain tendencies on a person. This does not mean, however, that we are not free. We are conditioned by these inclinations but are not determined by them. Personal experience tells us that we are free to make our choices, even if we might have certain inclinations towards one end or another. Precisely, it is part of human nature to be free, as Expressive Individualism recognizes by placing such a great emphasis on autonomy. Furthermore, as we saw above, all living beings tend to grow and develop until they reach their natural end, or telos. Living beings are perfected when they fulfill their nature and function. This is what is appropriate for them. In philosophy, this is referred to as the good of the being. This good is their end or purpose. And self-fulfillment is to achieve this end or purpose. What then is the good or end that human nature confers on a man?

In all living beings, including man, the good is to perfect one's capacities and faculties. What then are mankind's higher capacities and faculties—those that separate him from the animals? Unlike any other living being, man is rational and has a capacity for abstraction, to know a thing by its essence. A man can distinguish between a triangle and a four-sided figure such as a rectangle or a square. So can many animals. However, unlike any animal, a man can understand the difference between a figure with 300 sides and one with 301 sides, even though he can't imagine the two figures.

Man naturally communicates via complex language that is capable of expressing not just his biological states, but also a great number of other things: he can recount a story, write a poem, set out a theory, teach a class, etc. Animals, on the other hand, are capable of transmitting a limited number of messages that are always the same and are always linked to survival or biological needs. By his nature, man tends to choose ends that are higher than his biological needs. Unlike animals, he is not satisfied with the ends of the species (growth, survival, and reproduction). He is able to compose music, create art, write a novel, converse with people, go for a walk in nature, read a book, enjoy a movie, etc. He can choose to be a filmmaker, social worker, nurse, accountant, etc. He has more elevated goals: he can be motivated in his actions by a desire to grow in culture or by faith in God. Man is also the only animal that can attain transcendence. We can relate not only to other people, but we also believe that we can relate to a higher power, a divinity. Even if one claims that there is no divinity to relate to, it is undeniable that all human cultures, no matter how primitive or advanced, have always engaged in some form of relationship with what they perceive to be a higher power. This universal experience must then also form part of human nature. Because of all these qualities and characteristics, man possesses a unique dignity that no other animal can possess. In the Christian understanding of human nature, man's dignity lies in the fact that he is created in the image and likeness of God, and these qualities that separate him from the animals flow from that fact.

So, from the above we see that reason and free will are the highest faculties that man possesses. His reason and his free will are what separate him from the animals. Man is perfected when he uses his free will to lead a life according to reason. His reason discerns that certain ways of being and acting are more in accordance with his nature and so more conducive to his perfection. For example, he sees that he is perfected by life and health, knowledge of the truth, friendship, marriage, moral goodness, and the development of all the dimensions of his life so as to achieve harmony among all his faculties.

In seeking to lead a life according to reason and to engage in activities that lead to his perfection, he gradually develops a series of firm and deeply rooted habits and dispositions that help him to achieve that end. These habits and dispositions make it easier for him attain his true good and the harmony among all his faculties. They allow him to lead a full life, to reach self-fulfillment and attain true and lasting happiness. These habits and dispositions are what we refer to as the virtues.

In common parlance, virtues are character strengths. Examples of virtues are generosity, sincerity, loyalty, temperance, etc. Virtues make it easier to lead a fulfilled life with self-mastery and joy. The virtuous person naturally tends with all his faculties and powers to carry out actions that perfect him and lead to his good. He pursues the good and chooses it in concrete actions.

When a man chooses those goods that perfect him, he flourishes as a human being. And when a man chooses activities or objects that diminish him, the opposite happens, like the eagle in the cage. Our reason is able to discern between goods that perfect us and those that diminish us. With his free will, man can choose not to lead a life of virtue. He can choose other goals for his life and adopt other values. In Expressive Individualism autonomy reigns supreme. Nevertheless, it is a universal experience that exercising the virtues leads to happiness. People who are kind, generous, honest, prudent, loyal, and sincere are always happier than people who are mean, selfish, dishonest, imprudent, disloyal, and deceitful.

Natural Law[2]

Having seen that all men have a human nature and that that nature includes an end, or telos, we will now look at the question of natural law. The natural moral law (also called the natural law or the moral law) is an objective standard for what is morally right or wrong. It applies to all human beings, and it consists of those principles that are built into the design of human nature and lie at the roots of conscience. It consists of the basic moral truths themselves, based on human nature, which prescribe the pursuit and respect of what perfects us and forbid those things that diminish us. It can be known by everyone without the need to appeal to Divine Revelation.

The natural law is like the owner's manual of a car. The car does not function in a certain way because the owner's manual says so. On the contrary, the owner's manual states how the car will function because that is the way the car has been made. In a similar way, things are not right or wrong because the natural law says so. Rather, the natural moral law simply points out things that are right or wrong (good or bad for us) because of the way we are made (our human nature). Another analogy would be to compare the natural moral law to a road map. We can take New York City as a metaphor for the telos or proper goal of one's life. If one wishes to drive from Chicago to New York City, the map will show where New York City is located and what roads to take in order to drive there. The roads and New York City are not where they are because the map says so. On the contrary, the map is simply pointing out where they are in reality. In the same way, the natural moral law points out how to travel life's journey if one wishes to attain the goal of one's life. In other words, it is not a legal code superimposed on life, making it more difficult. It rather sets out the conditions that make authentic freedom and fruitful love possible. One can choose not to follow the natural law in the same way that one can choose not to follow the road map and the road that leads to New York City. But of course, by veering off the road, one

---

2   J. Budziszewski, *What We Can't Not Know* (Dallas: Spence Publishing Company, 2003); Peter Kreeft, *Making Choices* (Cincinnati: Servant Books, 1990). This discussion of Natural Law is inspired by the given citations.

is certainly going to end up in a ditch. And by following other roads, one may end up in Canada, of all places.

Even though the Church expounds a doctrine of natural law, it is not a uniquely Christian teaching. The Greek playwright Sophocles, as well as Plato, Aristotle, the Roman writer Cicero, and some Stoic philosophers, saw that there was such a thing as natural law. By this they meant an objective standard of morality, the basic principles of which all human beings can know by reason alone. For them, the knowledge of what is right and wrong is somehow written on the heart of every man. And since it is based on our human nature, they understood that that standard of morality applies to all human beings and is independent of cultural or other circumstances. As Cicero said:

> There is indeed a law, right reason, which is in accordance with nature, existing in all, unchangeable, eternal, commanding us to do what is right, forbidding us to do what is wrong. It has dominion over good men, but possesses no influence over bad ones. No other law can be substituted for it, no part of it can be taken away, nor can it be abrogated altogether. Neither the people or the senate can absolve from it. It is not one thing at Rome, and another thing at Athens: one thing to-day, and another thing to-morrow; but it is eternal and immutable for all nations and for all time.[3]

Cicero and the stoic philosophers believed that there is a natural law and that it is so binding that any human law made by a legislative entity that contradicts the natural law is invalid.

The founding fathers of the United States also believed in natural law, in universal and "self-evident" principles of morality, which the Declaration of Independence called "the laws of Nature and of Nature's God." Abraham Lincoln used natural law to ground his condemnation of the institution of slavery; Martin Luther King appealed to it to denounce racial discrimination.

Christianity inherited this understanding of a natural moral law from antiquity. The Apostle Paul states in his Epistle to the Romans that even though they have not received the written word of God, "when Gentiles who have not the law do by nature what the law requires, they are a law to themselves, even though they do not have the law."[4]

The Catholic Church embraced this notion of natural law, and its moral teaching reflects it and never contradicts it. But of course, since the Church has the benefit of Divine Revelation, it is able to delve deeper into the moral law and propound a richer, supernatural moral teaching that can lead man to

---

3   Cicero, *On the Commonwealth (De Re Publica)*, Book III, section XXII, paragraph 33.
4   Rom. 2:14-15 (Revised Standard Version, Second Catholic Edition).

far greater spiritual heights than is possible if one limits oneself to following natural morality.

When we say that the natural law is written on the heart, we do not mean that it is somehow innate, that somehow a baby is born with knowledge of it. Rather, what we mean is that the most basic principles of the natural law are known by reason and are indeed self-evident to reason. Once someone reaches the age of reason, he knows these basic principles. Once a child is able to understand the notions of right and wrong, of harm, of other people, of gratuitousness, then he immediately grasps that he should not gratuitously harm others. These most basic principles of morality are not provable; they are not derived from other principles. They are, as J. Budziszewski has said, "things we can't not know."[5]

What are these basic moral principles? The first and most basic one, of course, is to do good and avoid evil. But they would also include principles like Do not gratuitously harm another, do not deliberately take an innocent human life, take care of your family, render to others what is their due, do not have sex with another man's wife, do not steal what rightfully belongs to another, etc.

Our deep conscience, sometimes referred to as *synderesis*, is an interior witness of the foundational principles of morality. It cannot be erased or mistaken on these basic principles and is the same for every human being. It is knowledge, not a feeling. A man is able to violate one of these foundational principles and can even partially smother his guilt and remorse. But deep down he always knows that he is doing wrong, and this knowledge will invariably diminish him, affecting him in a negative way. Furthermore, these principles are absolute, objective, and universal, even though many people would prefer that they be relative, subjective, and particular. We can use the principle *Do not deliberately take an innocent human life* to illustrate this. It does not admit of exceptions. No circumstances can justify it. Our subjective feelings are irrelevant. The question of who is an innocent person is, of course, subject to debate. The man who breaks into your home and threatens to kill your family is not innocent. The terrorist engaged in an act of violence against innocent people is not innocent. The soldier who is part of an army that has unjustly invaded your country is not innocent. The question of who is an innocent person is not always clear. But, since our human nature is unchanging and universal, the principle is absolute, objective, and universal. Across space and time, every human being is aware of these principles. Every culture that has ever existed, from the most primitive to the most advanced, has held these principles. This, in itself, is proof that the natural law exists. Some would deny the previous statement, using different objections. We can look at the most common of them.

One objection is to contend that there are no objective moral truths. Rather, people have evolved to believe things like *taking care of your family is good* or

---

5   J. Budziszewski, *What We Can't Not Know* (Dallas: Spence Publishing Company, 2003).

killing the innocent is wrong because holding these beliefs is conducive to the survival of our species. This would explain why certain moral principles are universally held by humans without the need to posit the existence of any objective moral truths. However, this objection fails because when we examine the contents of our moral beliefs, we quickly find that morality is often opposed to the survival of our species. For example, consider adultery. Wouldn't it be better for the survival of our species if adultery was not only permitted but encouraged? Similarly, wouldn't it be better for the survival of our species if we simply neglected our parents once they age beyond their reproductive stage? Also, we often see examples of people making sacrifices to engage in charitable and philanthropic work to help people with whom they have no connection: people with disabilities and infirmities, for example, or people in far-off developing countries. Indeed, in an article entitled "The Limits of Evolutionary Explanations of Morality and Their Implications for Moral Progress," published in the journal *Ethics* at the University of Chicago, Professors Allen Buchanan and Russell Powell have convincingly refuted the theory that morality can be explained by evolution.[6]

Another objection is to say that *different cultures have different values*. For example, Nazi Germany was in favour of genocide, and cannibals think that eating other humans is fine. However, murder was still considered a crime in Nazi Germany, but the killing of the Jews was not considered murder. Rather, the Nazis saw their victims as both subhuman and guilty by virtue of their race. The cannibal likewise does not think that the people of the other tribe are humans. He would not kill and eat anyone from his own tribe. In other words, different cultures can get it wrong with respect to their application of these moral principles, but they still maintain the principles. No culture has ever existed that considered honesty to be immoral and dishonesty moral, or that courage is evil and cowardice a virtue. No culture has ever existed that condoned murder, theft, and adultery.

A third objection is to maintain that *in order to be free, I must create my own values. I am not free if moral values are imposed on me*. As we saw above, one is free to adopt whichever values one likes. But just as choosing values cannot change the laws of physics or biology, it can't change the natural law, which is based on our human nature. I can choose to adopt the value of free love and ignore the natural law prohibition against adultery, but that can't change the natural law, and in one way or another I will suffer the consequences of violating that law.

On the question of personal freedom, paradoxically, throughout modern history, it is precisely the concept of natural law that has enabled man to gain

---

6   Allen Buchanan and Russell Powell, "The Limits of Evolutionary Explanations of Morality and Their Implications for Moral Progress," *Ethics* 126, no. 1 (2015), 37-67, https://www.jstor.org/stable/10.1086/682188.

his freedoms and to have his human rights recognized. As we mentioned above, Martin Luther King opposed segregation by an appeal to an objective morality, and the abolitionists opposed slavery by an appeal to what is just by nature. In a similar way, when the Allied Powers tried the Nazis at Nuremberg, they based themselves on a concept of natural justice. Indeed, in modern times, appeals to natural law have been crucial to securing the betterment of mankind and securing greater justice.

It must also be borne in mind that, even though the natural law can be very specific in setting out the evils to be avoided, there are very few restrictions on how one is to do the good. Indeed, each one may pursue the good in the way that seems best to him with great freedom so long as he respects the natural law. A regime that seeks to impose excessive uniformity on the population in order to improve society does indeed violate natural law by denying each one the freedom to pursue the good in his own way.

Still another objection is to state that *considering the natural law as absolute, objective, and universal is uncompassionate and intolerant. Morality must be based on subjective motives and individual conscience. Relativism is humane and tolerant.* It should be immediately obvious that this objection opens the door to horrible abuses. If morality is purely subjective, depending on our feelings, then how does one condemn Hitler, who thought he was doing the world a favour by eliminating the Jewish people, or the Islamic terrorists, who thought that they were following their religion by destroying the World Trade Center? Without absolute, objective, and universal principles of morality, there is no way to judge anyone's actions, no matter how immoral they are.

A final objection is to say that these basic rules of morality are not derived from our human nature but are simply the result of a social contract. They are rules that all human societies have arrived at in order to live in peace and harmony with one another. They are practical and utilitarian principles, arrived at using our reason, but do not necessarily flow from our human nature. There are two answers to this objection. The first is to point out that there are certain actions that we all know are morally wrong and that no circumstances can justify. An example would be torturing a three-year-old child to death. That action is not wrong because a human law forbids it. It is not wrong because of a social consensus or a social contract. Indeed, even if a law were passed authorizing such a deed, it would still be inherently immoral because it violates the natural moral law. A second answer to this objection is that the social consensus does not always work. If there is no natural law, then the majority in a democracy can elect a government that will disenfranchise and even persecute a minority. In 1933, the Nazis came to power in Germany as the result of a valid election and on a blatantly anti-Semitic and hence immoral platform. The social consensus was persecution of the Jewish people.

Today, in the United States, entire classes of people have lost the most basic of human rights, the right to life. This includes foremost babies in the wombs of their mothers. These are the most innocent and most vulnerable members of society. They deserve all the protection of the law. And yet, since abortion was legalized in the United States, over sixty million innocent children have been killed through abortion in the U.S. alone. And there is an increasing movement in the U.S. to allow for the killing of babies born with disabilities. At the other end of the spectrum of human life, euthanasia is being used to kill the elderly. Although euthanasia is only supposed to be practiced with the consent of the patent, in Belgium, over half of the patients over 80 years old who are euthanized are not asked for their consent.[7]

It is true that most democracies have embedded the protection of human rights in their constitutions to prevent any abuse of power. But as we have just seen, they are frequently ineffective. This is often because they are so vaguely worded that the courts have a great latitude to decide if and how the protection of human rights applies in given cases. The first proof that there is such a thing as natural law was an appeal to universal human experience. Every sane person without exception can discern these basic moral principles. And throughout history, there has never been a culture, no matter how primitive or advanced, that did not hold these principles.

A second proof of natural law can be gleaned from its consequences. Since a violation of natural law is naturally bad for us, it will always carry some negative effect. We reap what we sow. This can be seen most obviously in addictions. The person who violates the natural law by drinking excessively, doing drugs, or watching pornography ends up addicted and loses a good part of his freedom. But this can be seen in other, less obvious examples. Those who offend others end up being disliked by everyone. Those who betray their friends will end up lonely, with no friends. Those who live by violence usually die violently. Those who don't tell the truth lose everyone's trust.

Extramarital sex can be used as an illustration. The woman might become pregnant, and the father will often leave her alone to raise her child on her own. Men who engage in casual sex see women as objects to satisfy their lust, and they lose their ability to love—to give oneself totally to another in a permanent, exclusive, and life-affirming relationship. Another negative consequence of extramarital sex is poverty because single mothers often have to raise their children on their own. Because they are raised without a father, male teenagers frequently end up in jail or addicted, or drop out of school or in depression. Venereal disease is far more common when casual sex is practiced. Also common is child abuse by live-in boyfriends who resent the presence of children whom they have not fathered themselves.

---

7   Raphael Cohen-Almagor, *Journal of Medical Ethics* 41, no. 8 (2015): 625-629.

These negative consequences of extramarital sex and of the other violations of natural law are not the reason that they are wrong. They would be wrong even if a solution could be found to avoid the negative effects. The fundamental negative effect that can never be overcome is that by engaging in conduct that violates the natural law, one is failing to thrive in a truly human way. One is failing to lead a happy, fulfilled, and meaningful life.

In summary, we can see that the existence of the natural law is evident both from the fact of universal human experience and from the natural negative consequences of violating that law. And the basic principles of that law can be known by everyone. They are things that we simply can't not know.

Chapter 5

Christianity's Contribution to Western Civilization

We saw in Chapter 4 that, contrary to the claims of Expressive Individualism, the natural moral law does indeed exist and its basic principles are known to everyone.

The next argument that the Christian can make is to show that the advances that Expressive Individualism claims for itself actually derive from Christianity and that even many of the elements of Expressive Individualism itself, such as autonomy, the spirit of rational inquiry, equality, human rights, and others, have their origin in Christianity. It is true that Expressive Individualism has a complex intellectual pedigree and, as we saw in Chapter 3, has adopted elements from Enlightenment thinkers, modern and contemporary philosophers, and other sources. And yet, as we trace back that pedigree, it becomes clear that many of the elements of Expressive Individualism find their origin in notions and insights that were first put forward by Christianity. Thanks to Christianity, these notions became imbedded in Western culture and civilization. They have now been severed from their Christian roots and distorted by the holders of Expressive Individualism, but their origin lies in Christianity. To illustrate this we will do a brief survey of Christianity's contribution to Western civilization and show how its insights and achievements form the basis of Expressive Individualism.

Christianity's Contribution to Western Civilization

Over the centuries, Europe and later North America have been responsible for what we view as some of the major achievements of the modern world. These would include the scientific revolution, the industrial revolution, and the technological revolution; the founding and development of the universities; the development of human rights, women's rights, and the abolition of slavery; great advances in literacy, health care, limited government, constitutional government, and the rule of law; the separation of church and state; the development of free market economics; and the development of social welfare systems, to name the most salient.

As will become clear below, these achievements all began and developed only in cultures that understood themselves to be Christian. It is true that some other cultures made scientific discoveries or had inklings of the insights that Christianity gifted to Western civilization and eventually to the rest of the world. But in those cultures, these scientific discoveries were always stillborn and petered out, and many other insights that thinkers in other civilizations arrived at never became embedded in their culture. It is only in cultures that understood themselves to be Christian that we witness a formal and sustained scientific inquiry over centuries and still continuing today. And it was only due to the insights that Christianity arrived at that the great achievements mentioned above took place. And the reason why this took place in Christian cultures, as we shall now see, has everything to do with Christianity. From its very beginnings, Christianity introduced some key insights into our world, without which none of these advances would have been possible.

Of course, no society in history has even been entirely Christian. Christians, like everyone else, are sinners, and indeed, every society is racked by sin. The Church has always had to be counter-cultural. When we speak about a Christian culture or a culture that understood itself to be Christian, we do not mean a society in which the Christian faith was perfectly lived. No such society is possible. It is rather a society informed by Christian principles and in which Christianity is held up as an ideal, even though that ideal is not lived up to in practice.

At the beginning of the millennium, a member of the Chinese Academy of Social Sciences spoke about how this institution tried to account for the success of the West to date. He stated the following:

> One of the things we were asked to look into was what accounted for the success, in fact, the pre-eminence of the West all over the world. We studied everything we could from the historical, political, economic and cultural perspective. At first, we thought it was because you had more powerful guns than we had. Then we thought it was because you had the best political system. Next we focused on your economic system. But in the past twenty years, we have realized that the heart of your culture is your religion: Christianity. That is why the West is so powerful. The Christian moral foundation of social and cultural life was what made possible the emergence of capitalism and then the successful transition to democratic politics. We don't have any doubt about this."[1]

It is noteworthy that this quote is not from a religious leader or some religious think tank. The Chinese Academy of Social Sciences forms part of the Chinese Communist government, which is officially atheistic.

---

1   David Aikman, *Jesus in Beijing: How Christianity Is Transforming China and Changing the Global Balance of Power*, (Washington: Regnery, 2003).

Science

We can begin with science. Many Expressive Individualists contend that science was only able to develop and flourish once it had broken free from control by the medieval church. Free from superstition and using reason and the scientific method, modern man has carried out the scientific revolution, the industrial revolution and the technological revolution. Science has thus been able to eliminate many diseases, extend life spans, lower infant mortality, and raise standards of living, lifting millions out of poverty. Yet, all these advances would have been impossible without certain key insights that Christianity introduced. We will have a brief look at four of them:

1. The first insight is contained in the very first words of the Bible: "In the beginning, God created the heavens and the earth" (Genesis 1:1). This first insight is that the world, the universe, is not divine. The universe is not God. God created the universe. But he is transcendent. He is outside the universe.

   Most primitive religions believed that the world, or parts of it, was divine. Nature was sacred (Mother Nature or Gaia). There were sacred ponds, sacred oaks, etc. The sun, moon, and stars, as well as natural phenomena, were considered gods. If one believes that the world is divine, then he doesn't experiment on it. He worships it and sacrifices to it the way primitive religions did.

2. A second key insight of Christianity is that the world is intelligible. With our reason, we can understand it. And why is it intelligible? Because it was created by a Great Intelligence. God is not some thing. He is Someone. He is a personal God. And as Creator, he has left his mark of intelligibility on every detail of the world.

   Now one may object that it is abundantly obvious that the universe is subject to the laws of physics and that these can be understood by our reason. However, prior to Christianity. this idea simply did not take root in any non-Western civilization. There was no reason to suppose that such laws existed.

   This notion is an inheritance from Greek philosophy. Some early Greek philosophers taught that reality exists objectively, is accessible to the intellect, and can be known as it is in itself. They also understood that there is a rational purpose behind the order in the universe and that this purpose is somehow related to the good towards which everything, including man's soul, is oriented. And they came to realize that the source of this good transcends the material world. As Plato has Socrates say: "The world is the product of a mind which sets everything in order and produces each individual thing in the way that is best for it."[2]

---

2 *Phaedo*, 99d

These insights of the ancient Greek philosophers were restricted to a very small group of intellectuals who were considered rather quirky by the general population. Their ideas were accordingly never espoused by the general public.

Christianity adopted these insights from the Greek philosophers, purifying them, developing them, and imbedding them in Western civilization. Christianity taught that the universe had been created by a rational God and that he had left the imprint of his rationality on his creation.

Not even the high cultures of ancient Greece, China, and the medieval Islamic world were able to effect the scientific revolution that took place in Christian Europe, because they all lacked the concept of an all-powerful, personal, and rational Creator. Ancient Chinese culture, for example, explained the world in terms of Yin and Yang, and they developed philosophy, medicine, and science based on this theory. But lacking the notion of a rational God these attempts never led to sustained development in these fields.[3]

And as Robert Reilly explains in his book, *The Closing of the Muslim Mind*,[4] a 9th century school of Islamic thought (the Mu'tazilites) effected a synthesis of faith and reason similar to the one that medieval philosophers achieved within Christianity. They contended that Islam should be subject to rational analysis, and conform to the demands of human reason. They were opposed by the Ash'arites, who insisted on complete subjection to the will of God and who considered any claim that Allah is subject to reason as blasphemous. For example, when faced with contradictory passages in the *Qu'ran*, the Mu'tazilites held that they should be logically analyzed in order to arrive at the truth. The Ash'arites, on the contrary, held that if Allah wishes to be contradictory, we should not question his will. So, the principle of non-contradiction, the most basic principle of rational thought, was rejected. As Reilly goes on to show, the Ash'arites triumphed over the Mu'tazilites, thereby instilling in Islamic thought a disregard towards philosophical rigour, rational analysis, and scientific exploration.

St. John begins his Gospel with the words "In the beginning [of the cosmos] was the Word [Logos, mind, reason, thought, wisdom,

---

3   Joseph Needham, *Science and Civilization in China Vol. 1*, (Cambridge: Cambridge University Press, 1954), 581; Stacy Trasancos, "The Stillbirth of Science in China," *Strange Notions*, August 1, 2014. https://strangenotions.com/the-stillbirth-of-science-in-china-2/; Stacy Trasancos, "Fr. Jaki and the Stillbirths of Science," *Catholic Education*, November 13, 2014. https://www.catholiceducation.org/en/science/faith-and-science/fr-jaki-and-the-stillbirths-of-science.html#:~:text=Fr.%20Stanley%20L.%20Jaki%20used%20the%20phrase%20stillbirths,Christianity.%20Jaki%20was%20aware%20it%20could%20evoke%20resentment.

4   Robert Reilly, *The Closing of the Muslim Mind* (Wilmington: ISI Books, 2010).

intelligence, idea, law, order, purpose, design], and the Word was with God, and the Word was God."[5]

Because God is a great intelligence, He acts rationally, and His rationality is reflected in His creation. There is an intelligible order, physical laws governing the universe, and we can understand that order and those laws because God made us in His image and likeness with a rational mind and so with the capacity to gain some understanding of Him and His intelligent order. We give glory to God by seeking to understand his creation.

Based on this insight, the Catholic Church founded the first universities in Europe in the Middle Ages.[6] The university was a new phenomenon in European history. Nothing like it had existed in ancient Greece or Rome. The first universities in Paris, Bologna, and Oxford, originated as far back as the late 12th century.

The Catholic Church founded the universities because it believed in the unity of truth, that God's creation was intelligible, and that the search for truth by our God given reason was worthwhile and attainable. This unity of truth was understood to mean that all branches of knowledge form a unity and their relationship to each other could be grasped, above all in light of Theology, which was considered the Queen of Sciences.

Thus, the first European universities offered a classical course of study. They taught theology, but they also taught non-theological subjects such as philosophy, medicine, law, natural science, rhetoric, grammar, astronomy, mathematics, music, etc.

Medieval universities prepared the way for the scientific revolution by training the intellect of Western Europe in the sense of order and in the principle of causality. Indeed, the commitment to reason and rational argument and the overall spirit of rational inquiry that characterized the first universities amounted to a gift from the Catholic Church to the modern world.

Even though we think of the scientific revolution as something beginning in the 17th century, impressive technological advances took place even in Christian Europe's High Middle Ages (1100–1300). The astrolabe, mechanical timepieces, more effective gears

---

5   Jn. 1:1 (Revised Standard Version, Second Catholic Edition).

6   Furhan Findikli, "Rethinking Ancient Centers of Higher learning: Madrasa in a Comparative-Historical Perspective," *British Journal of Educational Studies 7*, no. 2 (2021): 129-144. https://www.tandfonline.com/doi/full/10.1080/00071005.2021.1901853. There were universities in the Muslim world prior to those established by the Church in Europe. There were, however, significant differences between those institutions and the Christian universities. Their main purpose was to study Islamic law, and the natural or rational sciences were included as ancillaries and only in so far as they served the study of Islamic sciences. Islamic advances in astronomy, medicine, mathematics, and optics from the 8th to the end of the 13th centuries took place in hospitals and observatories rather than in their universities.

for windmills and water mills, advances in wagons and carts, the shoulder harness for beasts of burden, a new type of rudder that would allow ships to venture into the ocean, eyeglasses and magnifying glasses, smelting of iron, ironwork, stone cutting, and new principles of architecture. Historian Jean Gimpel was so impressed by this that he wrote a book in 1976 called *The Industrial Revolution of the Middle Ages.*[7]

Almost all the giants of the scientific revolution were Christians who had studied in the church-sponsored universities and who took their Christian faith seriously. They saw no incompatibility between their Christian faith and their study of science. On the contrary, they saw their scientific discoveries as a way to give glory to their Creator.

Some of these giants of the scientific revolution include

Copernicus, who formulated the heliocentric model of the universe was a Catholic Church official in Poland.

Kepler, who discovered the laws of planetary motions, was a devout Christian who saw his work as a way of giving glory to God.

Galileo was a devout Catholic all his life, even after his run-in with the Catholic Church.

Blaise Pascal (a mathematician who invented probability theory) was a devout Catholic who wrote a book on the spiritual life.

Newton (calculus, gravity, the three laws of motion) wrote a book reflecting his strong faith in Christianity.

Gregor Mendel (the father of the science of genetics) was a Catholic monk.

Father Georges Lemaitre, who first worked out the theory of the Big Bang, was a Catholic priest.

Michael Faraday was a pioneer in electricity and magnetism and also a firm Christian.

Renowned physicist **William Thomson Kelvin** was president of a Bible society in Scotland.

Max Planck, the father of quantum theory, came from a family of theologians.

Louis Pasteur was a Catholic, as were **Alexander Fleming** and **Father Roger Boscovich**, a founder of modern atomic theory.

Father Jean Picard was a 17th century priest who was the first person to determine the size of the earth to a reasonable degree of accuracy.

Father Giovanni Battista Riccioli was a 17th century Jesuit astronomer and the first person to measure the rate of acceleration of a free-falling body.

---

7   Jean Gimpel, *The Medieval Machine: The Industrial Revolution of the Middle Ages* (New York: Henry Holt & Company, Inc, 1976).

Father Francesco Grimaldi was a 17th Century Jesuit priest who discovered the diffraction of light.

The leading astronomers of Europe from the 17th century were the Jesuits (a Catholic religious order), and their observatory was in the Vatican, the headquarters of the Catholic Church.

From this brief overview it becomes obvious that the so-called War between Science and Religion is no more than a myth. The origins of this myth lie in the late 19th century, and especially in the work of two men: John William Draper and Andrew Dickson White. The work of both men has since been discredited, and today no serious historian of science embraces this thesis.

Lawrence Principe is Professor of both Chemistry and the History of Science, Medicine, and Technology at Johns Hopkins University. He has stated that the Catholic Church was "probably the largest single and longest term patron of science in history"[8]

3. A third insight of Christianity is that God created the universe for man, and He gave man the mission or mandate to subdue it and be its master.

God blessed them, saying "Be fruitful and multiply, and fill the earth and subdue it; and have dominion over the fish of the sea and over the birds of the air and over every living thing that moves upon the earth."[9]

If one understands that the universe was made for man and that mankind is called to subdue it, then one makes the effort to understand it and control it. It gives man an impetus to harness the forces of nature and to be a proper steward of creation, preserving it for future generations.

4. The fourth insight of Christianity is the linearity of time and history and the notion of progress. The Church understood that the universe had a beginning, that it will have an end, and that it has a purpose: the glory of God and the salvation of men. The notion of progress was born. Most non-Christian religions saw time as cyclical and without purpose or meaning and believed that our lives are subject to an implacable fate.

Because it understood the notion of progress, the Catholic Church became the only institution in Europe that showed consistent interest in the preservation and cultivation of the advances made in human knowledge. Much of the learning of Ancient Greece and Rome was preserved by medieval Catholic monks copying

---

8   Ronald L. Numbers, ed., *Galileo Goes to Jail: And Other Myths about Science and Religion*, (Cambridge: Harvard University Press, 2009), 102.

9   Gen. 1:28 (Revised Standard Version, Second Catholic Edition).

manuscripts. Without them, our knowledge of ancient history, philosophy, literature, etc., would be much poorer.

Without these four insights science cannot develop. In summary:

- If you think the world is God, you worship it; you don't experiment on it.
- And if you don't believe that the world is intelligible, if you don't believe that it can be understood, you don't try to understand it—you don't pursue science either.
- If you understand that the universe was made for man and that mankind is called to subdue it, then you make the effort to understand it and control it.
- If you understand that the universe has a beginning, an end, and a purpose, and that you are called to fulfill that purpose, then you work hard to do so.

All of this made conditions ripe for the scientific revolution, the industrial revolution, and the technological revolution. And in large part, this is why they took place in Europe and nowhere else.

Faith and Reason

In addition to the gift of the scientific revolution, another contribution of Christianity to Western civilization was the quest for truth through a spirit of rational inquiry and the wedding of Faith and Reason. Expressive Individualists hold that we do not need faith to build civilization. It is by reason using science that man has conquered nature, made scientific and technological breakthroughs, and improved life expectancy, health, and the standard of living. They consider reason to be powerful, universal, and reliable and maintain that most problems can be solved by the use of reason. We should consequently lead a life according to reason without any need for faith. As we saw above, however, it was the Catholic Church's insight into the intelligibility of the universe and its founding of the universities that established the spirit of rational inquiry that has characterized Western Civilization and made the scientific revolution possible. Furthermore, the Catholic Church has always rejected superstition in religious matters and has used reason to reject it. In fact, even before the time of Christ, in Genesis, the very first book of the Bible, we see an attack on superstition.

In the early creation mythologies of the Middle East the world is said to have begun with a primeval chaos and a multiplicity of gods warring among themselves. The very first words of the Bible reject this irrational fantasy: "In the beginning God created the heavens and the earth." The God of the Old Testament is the one and only God. He creates with his word. And as we have seen, He is a rational God. Moreover, the Church banished the supernatural from the material world (sacred ponds, sun worship, etc.). From time immemorial, mankind had relied on witch doctors, soothsayers, and shamans to be intermediaries between the gods of nature and the community. In the Old Testament, for the first time in the history of humanity, such people are banned.[10] However, even though the Christian tradition has always promoted the use of reason to pursue the truth, it maintains that reason needs faith in order to attain the ultimate truths, i.e., truths about the meaning and purpose of life. So, the Catholic Church has always taught that with our reason, using philosophy rather than the empirical sciences, man can arrive at the knowledge of the existence of God without the help of revelation and can know some of his attributes. And by studying the natural law, man can build up a basic ethical system. But reason alone is like someone in a rowboat. He can discover some things but is limited and always has to stay close to shore. A man of faith, using his reason, has a large ship that allows him to put out into the deep and discover new lands. Faith enables him to know and experience so much more. For example, Catholic moral teaching is far richer and goes much deeper than basic natural law morality. As we saw in Chapter 1, it allows a man to lead a virtuous life in close communion with God.

The Church also maintains that God is both the author of the universe and of divine revelation. Since he is rational and can't contradict himself, there can be no incompatibility between faith and reason. Any apparent incompatibility is due to faulty theology or faulty use of reason. What is the problem with the position of the Expressive Individualist? What is the problem with wanting to lead a life strictly according to reason and denying the supernatural? The problem is that reason alone is inadequate, since it raises questions that it cannot answer on its own and to which only faith provides answers. Reason alone cannot provide the answers to the most basic questions of human existence: why does the universe exist and why are we here? What happens to our spirit after death? How can we know whether an action is right or wrong, whether a society is just or unjust? These are questions about our origin, our destiny, and the ultimate meaning and purpose of our existence. Each of us raises them at some point or other, and rather earlier than later in life. And by their very nature, these questions cannot be resolved using the scientific method, no matter how far science advances, since they are of a different order altogether.

Using philosophy, we can obtain some inkling to the answers. For example, the great philosophers Plato and Aristotle meditated on these matters and arrived at a concept of God and an understanding that the good life, the life that leads to human flourishing, was a life of virtue. But without divine revelation, their answers were bound to be incomplete, as was their concept of God. They certainly went a long way. Reason does not leave us completely destitute. But on the ultimate questions, it requires the help of faith. Pope St. John Paul II

10   Leviticus. 19:31, 20: 6, 20: 27, Deuteronomy 18: 10-12

articulated the Christian insight into this issue as follows:

> Faith and reason are like two wings on which the human spirit rises to
> the contemplation of truth; and God has placed in the human heart
> a desire to know the truth—in a word, to know himself—so that,
> by knowing and loving God, men and women may also come to the
> fullness of truth about themselves.[11]

We are hard-wired to seek the truth. We can't help asking these questions
about the origin, meaning, and purpose of our lives. Even young children ask
them without ever having been prompted to do so. And if we do not know
the meaning of our life, then how can we know what kind of life to lead? A
worldview based on reason alone can only answer the question by declaring
that our life has no inherent meaning. Each person decides the meaning of his
own life.

Faith, on the other hand, provides an answer, from which reason can then
draw out some implications. Once our reason knows through faith why we
are here, it can draw conclusions on how we ought to live. The same may be
said about the most radical philosophical question that can ever be asked: why
is there something rather than nothing? This is another question that simply
cannot be ignored because, whether we like it or not, the way we live necessarily
implies a response.

To ignore the question usually leads to unwittingly adopting the default
stance of the time in which one is living. The Expressive Individualist who
doesn't know the meaning of his existence must still decide how to lead his life.
So he will often adopt the prevailing life-style, fashions, fads, and ideologies of
his culture, and as G.K. Chesterton said, he becomes subject to "the degrading
servitude of being a child of his age."[12]

Without faith, the Expressive Individualist lacks a proper moral compass.
A proper system of ethics must be grounded in an anthropology that is based
on a correct concept of what man is. And it is only Christianity that provides
that concept. Without it, even a system as brilliant as Aristotle's virtue ethics is
deficient in some ways. Since the Modern Self rejects natural law and denies that
man's life has an objective end, the best that he can do is to ground ethics in the
Golden Rule and the Do No Harm principle and rely on the social consensus
for what is permissible. However, these principles are inadequate, as we shall see
below when we look at Christianity's contribution to ethics.

In summary, Christianity has always encouraged the use of reason to pursue

---

11   John Paul II, *Fides et Ratio*, encylical letter, September 14, 1998, https://www.vatican.va/
content/john-paul-ii/en/encyclicals/documents/hf_jp-ii_enc_14091998_fides-et-ratio.html.

12   Gilbert Chesterton, *Twelve Modern Apostles and Their Creeds*, (New York: Duffield &
Company, 1926), 19.

the truth, and in this way it was responsible for the spirit of rational inquiry that has characterized the West. Its wedding of faith and reason provided deep insights into the human condition that reason was then able to explore. This wedding of faith and reason also set out clear ethical limits as to what is permissible by reason. Expressive Individualism has torn reason away from faith and is increasingly engaging in activities directly opposed to man's dignity, such as abortion, embryonic stem cell research, genetic manipulation, human cloning, etc.

Equality, Human Rights, Women's Rights and the Abolition of Slavery

By human rights, we understand rights that each human being possesses by virtue of being human. They are not rights granted to individuals by the state. They pre-exist the state. A right is a moral entitlement or a morally justified claim to have or obtain something, to act in a certain way, or to be free from certain actions. Examples would be the right to life, the right to religious liberty, and the right to security of one's person.

The ancient world of Greece and Rome held that citizens had civic rights, such as the right to vote, the right of assembly, etc. These rights were granted by the laws or the constitution of the state and were not enjoyed by slaves and others who were not citizens. As we saw in Chapter 4, the ancient world of Greece and Rome also arrived at a notion of natural law. However, even though the world of antiquity developed the notion of natural law, it did not arrive at the concept of human dignity and so failed to develop a theory of natural rights or human rights. As Kyle Harper has stated: "None of the classical political regimes, nor any of the classical philosophical schools, regarded human beings as universally free and incomparably worthy creatures. Classical civilization, in short, lacked the concept of human dignity."[13] Indeed, it was not until the Middle Ages that Christian thinkers developed the concept of human rights. In order to do so, another key insight was required, which was basically that all men and women are equal. It was the Christian teaching on equality that eventually led to the development of the concept of human rights.

The creation of humanity by God is described in Genesis as follows:

> Then God said, "Let us make man in our image, after our likeness; and let them have dominion over the fish of the sea, and over the birds of the air, and over the cattle, and over all the earth, and over every creeping

13   Kyle Harper, "Christianity and the Roots of Human Dignity in Late Antiquity," in *Christianity and Freedom, Volume I: Historical Perspectives*, ed. Timothy Samuel Shah and Allen D. Hertzke, (Cambridge: Cambridge University Press, 2016), 143.

thing that creeps upon the earth." So God created man in his own image, in the image of God he created him; male and female he created them.[14]

Both men and women were created in the image and likeness of God. This meant that both men and women share the same human nature and are therefore equal and possessed of a great dignity. This radical equality of all humans was expressed by St. Paul in the following words: "There is neither Jew nor Gentile; there is neither slave nor freeman; there is neither male or female. For you are all one in Christ."

Some of the Stoics in Ancient Rome held to the equality of men and women based on the fact that both were rational. However, the Stoics lacked sufficient influence and so were unable to embed this insight into the culture. How did the teaching on equality allow thinkers to move from the concept of Natural Law to that of Natural Rights or Human Rights?

Christianity understood that man is a being created in the image and likeness of God, redeemed by the precious blood of Christ, and as such, men are bearers of a profound, inherent, and equal dignity. All men, regardless of their religion, are called by God to actualize the full likeness of God imprinted on them at creation by following the Natural Law. Basing themselves on this, medieval Canon lawyers worked out the conclusion that each man and woman must be endowed with certain inalienable rights in keeping with their dignity and entitling them to follow the natural law.[15]

The development of this concept of human rights received a great impetus from the 16th century debates over the rights of the Indians in the New World. The early colonists began enslaving and otherwise mistreating the indigenous peoples of the New World. This was denounced by Catholic missionaries, and in response to this outcry, King Phillip II of Spain organized a series of theological debates in Spain to see whether this treatment of the indigenous peoples was truly immoral. In these debates, it became clear that the Indians were human and so enjoyed the same human rights as others.[16] By the beginning of the 17th century, a complete theory of Human Rights had been expounded by Catholic theologians and Canon lawyers. However, the Catholic Church's human rights theory was carefully circumscribed by limits emanating from Natural Law. Each person has a duty to act according to Natural Law if he is to lead a fully human life and so actualize the full likeness of God imprinted on him at creation. It is from this duty that human rights are seen to flow. They are not seen as our private property to use as we please, but as something that allows us to follow the natural law. The Church understood that man has a specific nature and is

---

14   Gen. 1:26-27 (Revised Standard Version, Second Catholic Edition).
15   Brian Tierney, *The Idea of Natural Rights* (Atlanta: Scholars Press, 1997), Chapters I-VII.
16   Tierney, *The Idea of Natural Rights*, Chapter XI.

part of a universal order. Christian thinkers preferred the term Natural rights rather than human rights because it stresses a grounding in human nature. It connects the concept with the older idea of natural law. The ultimate grounds of morality are not human rights but human nature created by God. So one has a human right to act in accordance with the Natural Law.

The basic human rights were limited to those things that one needed in order to lead a fully human life according to the purpose of one's life as it was given to us by God. They were seen as the right to life and the security of one's person. The right not to be enslaved. They included freedom of religion and conscience, the right to marry someone of the opposite sex, and the rights of parents to educate and raise their children. The right to equality before the law and the right of one and one's family to be free from undue interference by the state or others. The right to work to support one's family. This Christian insight into the equality of all men and women and the consequent principle of human rights led eventually to the abolition of slavery.[17] If all men and women are created equal, one cannot own another human being. The woman's rights movement also would not have happened without this insight and the work of the Catholic Church over the centuries to ensure equal rights for women.[18]

In Expressive Individualism, the notion of human rights has undergone a transformation. It has been wrested from its grounding in natural law (which the Expressive Individualist does not believe in) and been distorted and placed at the service of the concept of Autonomy. So it is now considered that everyone has a human right to pursue his own life project and that each member of an identity group has rights, not just as a human being, but as a member of that group. Indeed, more often than not, human rights claims are made for social and economic privileges rather than for basic human rights. Human rights would now be considered to include many that are directly opposed to natural law, such as the right to change one's gender, to no-fault divorce, abortion on demand, same-sex marriage, euthanasia, etc. Yet this new understanding of human rights would not have been possible without the work of the Catholic Church over the centuries in establishing the principle that all men and women are equal, refining the notion of natural law, originating the concept of human rights, and ensuring that these principles were imbedded in Western culture.

17 Pierre Bonnassie, *From Slavery to Feudalism in South-Western Europe*; Joel Panzer, *The Popes and Slavery*, (New York: Alba House, 1996).

18 Francis Martin, *The Feminist Question*, (Grand Rapids: Eerdmans, 1994); Regine Pernoud, *Women in the Days of the Cathedrals*, (San Francisco: Ignatius Press, 1998).

Freedom and Autonomy

Christianity teaches that we are self-directed and self-determining persons and
so ultimately responsible for our choices. Although some of the Stoics and other
Greek and Roman philosophers had valid insights into the nature of freedom,
their insights failed to permeate the culture of antiquity. The Hebrew prophets
articulated this notion of freedom and Christianity developed it. In addition
to the concept of free will and moral responsibility, Christianity also developed
another insight into freedom linked to the idea of purpose. In the Gospel of St.
John, Christ says that "the truth will make you free."[19] The truth that sets us free
is the truth about our condition as created and redeemed beings made in God's
image and likeness and called to eternal happiness in heaven. It is the truth
about why we have been created and God's purpose for us.

Christianity teaches that we are free so that we can choose the good in free
submission to the dictates of the Natural Law in order to flourish and be happy
in this life and the next: to fulfill our great potential, achieve the end for which
we were created, and become the kind of person we were meant to be, which is
the only way for us to be truly happy. The Stoics and other ancient philosophers
did have a certain grasp of this insight, but once again it was necessarily partial
and it failed to influence their culture. It was Christianity that introduced a
comprehensive understanding of freedom.

Christian moral teaching demonstrates that when we use our freedom
to choose the good, we end up by generating a series of habits or virtues
that confer on our freedom a facility to do the good. True moral freedom
does not consist in doing something because I feel like it, but in doing good
because I feel like it. Internal freedom is the absence of subjective restraints
or compulsions that might inhibit one from acting according to what one
knows to be good. This internal freedom is necessary for the perfection of
character. Internal freedom is lost by the inability or unwillingness to restrain
one's passions, impulses, or emotions. Addiction is a polite word for the loss
of internal freedom.

A person driven by impulses or passions is not internally free. He does what
he knows is unnecessarily harmful but has little internal restraint to stop himself.
He is a prisoner of his own whims and desires. So, self-discipline is needed to
maintain one's inner freedom. This helps to understand the Christian teaching
that freedom is compatible with the moral law. The moral law sets out the good
that I am called upon to do. It points us in the direction that we should follow
if we wish to lead a full life. And we exercise our freedom by freely choosing
to follow the moral law because we want the end to which it points. Far from

---

19   Jn. 8:32 (Revised Standard Version: Second Catholic Edition).

constituting a restriction of our freedom, the moral law enhances it by pointing out how to use our freedom correctly if we wish to thrive and be happy.[20]

Expressive Individualism has adopted the Christian understanding of humans as self-directed and self-determining persons but has separated this notion from its Christian roots in order to have it stand on its own. As we saw in Chapter 2, instead of understanding freedom as a means that allows us to make choices that lead us to our last end, Expressive Individualism maintains that our purpose and last end are not given to us. For Expressive Individualism, freedom, or autonomy, includes the ability to choose our purpose and last end and to change those choices as often as we want. It is the misidentification of freedom with the absence of external law or restraint. Hence any attempt by the government, a church, or an individual to impose values on others or in any other way to limit an individual's right to pursue his own life project is decried as an attack on the individual's rights and liberties. But this notion of autonomy could never have come about without Christianity's teaching on freedom as it developed over the centuries.

Human Dignity and the Right to Life

Christianity's insight into the equality of all men and women also meant that human life was sacred. The Church understood that each individual human person is unique and unrepeatable. Each one possesses an inherent worth and a great dignity. Each one is created in the image and likeness of God and called to a supernatural last end in heaven. No one may arrogate to himself the right to take the life of an innocent human being.

Once the Roman Empire became Christian, the Christian Emperors began to legislate in this direction. They outlawed infanticide, which had been common. Infants who were unhealthy or deformed had often been left out to die. Sons were needed for the army, but having more than one or two daughters was considered a liability. Many female infants had been left out to die as well. The Christian Emperors ended this practice.[21] In Roman law, masters also had the right to put their slaves to death. This practice, too, was ended by the Christian Emperors.[22]

At the same time, the Church's insight into equality and the right to life meant that life was sacred from the moment of conception to natural death.

---

20   Catechism of the Catholic Church, 2nd ed. (Vatican City: Vatican Press, 1997), 1730-1748. For a description of the Church's understanding of Freedom, see the given citation.

21   In A.D. 374, Christian Emperor Valentinian I decreed that parents must raise their children and that the killing of an infant was a capital offence.

22   Karl Bihlmeyer, Church History, Vol. 1, Christian Antiquity (Westminster: The Newman Press, 1968), 375.

The Catholic Church considers the unborn infant to be the most innocent and most defenseless of all, and so is entitled to the full protection of the law. It consequently considers abortion to be morally reprehensible. Furthermore, modern scientific research has borne out the Church's position. We now know that from every scientific point of view, from the moment of conception, the unborn infant possesses its own genetic make-up distinct from that of either parent and so possesses the essential attribute that defines a human being. This is why those who hold to Expressive Individualism have abandoned any scientific argument as to the nature of the unborn child and have rather opted for the criterion of autonomy. They maintain that one becomes a person and a beneficiary of human rights only once one is autonomous. And since the unborn child is not autonomous, it cannot benefit from the right to life. The Catholic Church also contends that, since life is a gift from God, no one may arrogate to himself the right to end another's life or even to end one's own. Therefore, it considers not only euthanasia but all suicide, including physician-assisted suicide, to be morally wrong.

Expressive Individualism has taken the Christian notion of the dignity of each person but separated it from its Christian foundation in order to make it stand on its own. This has resulted in the radical individualism of Expressive Individualism, which, as we saw in Chapter 2, leads to what at times is referred to as the imperial self, the sovereign individual, or the autonomous self. However, this autonomy is taken as a premise and is not based on any intellectually coherent foundation. It has only been possible to conceive of it as a result of the Christian tradition's teaching on equality and human dignity.

Tolerance

It is sometimes maintained that ancient Greece and Rome were tolerant societies and that it was Christianity that introduced intolerance to the West. The Christian martyrs of the first three centuries would certainly be surprised by that statement. Indeed, as Peter Garnsey has shown, that is not an accurate portrayal of tolerance in the world of antiquity.[23] The Athenians, for example, did not tolerate foreign gods. They executed Socrates for failing to acknowledge the city's gods and for introducing new deities. The Romans did sometimes absorb the gods of conquered peoples into their pantheon. However, this was seen as a way of appropriating them and neutralizing them as allies of the conquered nations. The fact is that anyone who refused to worship the gods of Rome was persecuted. It is true that the Romans extended sporadic tolerance to the Jews

23 Peter Garnsey, *Religious Toleration in Classical Antiquity* (Cambridge: Cambridge University Press, 2016).

in the Empire in recognition of the military help that the Jews had rendered. The edicts that allowed the Jews to worship according to their religion state that this is a privilege being granted and make no reference to religious pluralism. In fact, the arguments that were made in favour of religious freedom in the ancient world were made by Christians who were being persecuted for their religion.

What is the Christian understanding of tolerance? In the parable of the weeds in the 13th Chapter of the Gospel of Matthew, we are told that we should allow the weeds to grow in the field of the world together with the good seed in view of the harvest (the final judgment). Hence it is often more prudent not to repress moral and religious error in order to promote a greater good.

The greater good referred to is respect for the dignity of the person, and respect for the truth and for the way that the human intellect arrives at the truth. For the Christian, tolerance in no way implies that moral and religious truth is relative. As we saw above, the Christian Tradition teaches that moral and religious truth is objective, universal and absolute. It further teaches that man has an obligation to seek out and embrace this truth. As Vatican II stated:

> It is in accordance with their dignity as persons, beings endowed with reason and free will, and therefore privileged to bear personal responsibility, that all men should be at once impelled by their nature and bound by a moral obligation to seek the truth, especially religious truth. They are also bound to adhere to the truth, once it is known, and to order their whole lives in accord with the demands of the truth.[24]

The Christian understanding of tolerance always implies tolerating someone who is in error when repressing that error would cause greater harm than allowing it to continue. Seeking to force the truth on someone violates that person's dignity and thereby causes greater harm than his acceptance of the truth would bring about. And in any event, the truth cannot be imposed. It must be accepted willingly as truth.

Tolerance has to do with people rather than ideas. The Christian tolerates someone who professes error, but he does not embrace the error as such. And this tolerance is not indifference. His love for each person will move him to engage in a dialogue with those who are in error and to try to convince them, out of love for the truth and out of love for them and for the entire society, which can only profit from having more members living according to the truth about man. But the Christian will never try to impose the truth on anyone through coercion or violence.

---

24   Second Vatican Council, "Declaration on Religious Freedom, Dignitatis Humanae," December 7, 1965, sec. 2 (hereafter cited as DH), https://www.vatican.va/archive/hist_councils/ii_vatican_council/documents/vat-ii_decl_19651207_dignitatis-humanae_en.html.

Because of the political situation in the Middle Ages and early modern times, it was not possible to completely implement the teaching of Christ as to the separation of Church and State. The alliance between the two was so close that the legitimacy of the political leader (Emperor, king, duke, etc.) really depended on the order of Faith. The political leader held power by the grace of God and was anointed by a representative of the Church (the pope or bishop). Hence the state often enforced Church doctrine as in the Inquisition, the Wars of Religion, etc., leading to intolerance. But once the Catholic Church disentangled itself from the political power, it was the above understanding of tolerance that Christianity bequeathed to western civilization and which led to the creation of a pluralistic, peaceful, and tolerant society.

This Christian understanding of tolerance has been altered by Expressive Individualism. As we saw in Chapter 2, in Expressive Individualism moral truth is relative. It says that the only universal moral values are the Golden Rule and the Do No Harm principle. As long as one respects these two principles, one can adopt his or her own values and his or her own truth. Tolerance becomes simply respecting the choice of values others make so long as their actions do not harm others. And all such choices are equally valid. We should all be tolerant of our diversity. Thus, Expressive Individualism has separated the notion of tolerance from the notion of moral and religious truth. Because in Expressive Individualism there is almost no moral or religious truth, everyone's choices must be accepted and celebrated. It is now considered intolerant even to suggest that one's values are universally true or in any way superior to those of another. And the Christian concern for trying to lead others to the truth through dialogue is now considered by Expressive Individualism to be completely unacceptable.

Health Care and Charity

Another of the Church's insights was that Christians are called to treat others with charity, whether they are Christian or not. Christians are bound by Christ's new commandment: *love one another, even as I have loved you*[25] and many other admonitions of this type.

A major stimulus to the expansion of Christianity in the first centuries was this charity. From the very beginning, Christians cared for widows and orphans, the feeding and housing of the poor, medical care for the sick, the burying of the dead, etc. In the first centuries after Christ, when the plague struck a town, everyone would flee, except the Christians. They would stay and minister to

25 Jn. 13:34 (Revised Standard Version: Second Catholic Edition).

those who were sick, whether they were Christians or not. This selfless behaviour moved many pagans to become Christians.[26]

The first hospitals in Europe were started by the Catholic Church.[27] These were institutions with doctors who made diagnoses and prescribed remedies and where nursing provisions were available. In the ancient world, provisions were made to tend to wounded soldiers, and the rich could hire doctors to minister to them in their illness. In addition, the wealthy endowed public baths and games, but there was little concern for the poor and sick. Indeed, in the ancient world, to bestow mercy was considered a weakness and even a defect. Since it implied providing *unearned* assistance to another, it was considered to be opposed to the virtue of justice. It was also considered to be a mark of immaturity, a sign that one had not yet learned to master his emotions and his impulse to show compassion to the suffering.

Of course, men have always been cruel to one another, and Christians have been no exception to this rule. The key advance represented by the Christian teaching on charity was that now it was a commandment to treat others with mercy and compassion, to alleviate suffering, and to help those in need. Although Christians still engage in cruelty, it is clear that the practice is sinful. This lies in stark contrast with the ancient world, where the norm was indifference to the suffering of another, where cruelty could often be justified, and where the punishments decreed by the law (such as crucifixion) could be unspeakably harsh. Thanks to the influence of Christianity, most governments today see it as an important part of their duty to ensure that the more needy people in society are cared for: health care, unemployment insurance, shelters, welfare systems, and other elements of the social safety net.

This teaching on charity has had a major beneficial effect on the world. The Catholic Church today manages 26% of the world's health care. It operates 18,000 clinics, 16,000 senior's homes, and 5,500 hospitals. Secular governments in industrialized countries have ejected the Church from many of its health care institutions and replaced it with government-run care, so most of the Catholic Church's health care institutions are located in developing countries. It manages 25% of the health care in India, even though less than 2% of the population is Christian, and 25% of the health care in Africa.[28]

---

26 Rodney Stark, *The Rise of Christianity* (Princeton: Princeton University Press, 1996), Chapter 4.

27 Gary B. Ferngren, *Medicine and Health Care in Early Christianity* (Baltimore: Johns Hopkins University Press, 2009).

28 John Agnew, "Deus Vult: The Geopolitics of Catholic Church," *Geopolitics* 15, no. 1 (2010): 39–61. https://www.researchgate.net/publication/248944969_Deus_Vult_The_Geopolitics_of_the_Catholic_Church; Robert Calderisi, *Earthly Mission - The Catholic Church and World Development*, (Padstow: TJ International Ltd, 2013), 40; "Catholic hospitals comprise one quarter of world's healthcare, council reports," *Catholic News Agency*, February 10, 2010. https://www.catholicnewsagency.com/news/18624/catholic-hospitals-comprise-one-quarter-of-worlds-healthcare-council-reports.

Christianity's teaching on charity is based on the fact that the very purpose of our life is to be transformed in Christ, to become identified with Christ, and to imitate him. And Christ's whole life was one of love. Love for His Father, God, and love for all men to the point of dying for them. He never sought Himself in anything that He did. So to be another Christ is to love our Father God above all things and to love one another as Christ loved us—completely, without any limits.

Many Expressive Individualists have a concern and compassion for the poor, the sick, the homeless, refugees, orphans, those with disabilities, etc. It was Christianity that introduced the notion into the world that this concern and compassion is something good and virtuous. However, once again, Expressive Individualism's understanding of concern and compassion for the needy has been removed from its Christian foundation. Hence, most Expressive Individualists see concern and compassion for the needy as something good, but they base it more on a general sentiment of compassion and not on any intellectual foundation.

Limited Government and the Rule of Law

Constitutional government and the rule of law play a crucial role in the just functioning and economic prosperity of a society. As history has repeatedly borne out, without them, a society easily falls into economic collapse as well as tyranny and a failure to respect human rights and individual liberties.

Constitutional government is by definition limited government. By this term, we mean that the authority of the sovereign or the government is not unlimited or arbitrary. It is not above the law and can only exercise those powers conferred on it by the constitution and the law. In addition, there is a sphere over which it has no authority, including the respect for human rights, which are usually enshrined in the constitution. In a constitutional government the balance of powers among the executive, legislative, and judicial branches of government is set out. It is thus a means to constrain any arbitrary exercise of power by the government.

By the rule of law, we mean that all people and institutions are subject to and accountable to law that is fairly applied and enforced. It is the idea that the law applies to everyone and everyone is equal before the law. Both the human rights and the civil rights of the citizens are protected. A corollary of the rule of law is the legal protection of private property rights. The Catholic Church taught that human freedom, human dignity, and the right of the labourer to his hire all implied the right to private property. And one of the roles of government was to protect that right. The rule of law also includes the principle that the police and the courts function independently and fairly, that contracts can be enforced before the courts, that the vote of legislators cannot be bought, etc.

Expressive Individualists consider constitutional government and the rule of law as achievements of their secular liberal worldview. However, as we shall now see, they first arose in Christian nations as a result of the Church's insights and teaching on the nature and importance of Justice and divine authority.

The jurists of the Roman Empire had had a genius for law. With the fall of the Empire, however, the corpus of Roman Law had been largely lost, and law in Western Europe became generally based on barbaric and primitive principles; for example, trial by battle and ordeal, and generally forcing people accused of crimes to undergo tests based on superstition and which had no relation to the crimes they were accused of. There was nothing resembling modern rules of evidence or rational legal procedures.

Beginning in the late 11th and the 12th centuries, the Catholic Church began to assert its authority in several ways (the founding of the universities, the Crusades, the Inquisition, the Investiture Struggle, etc.). One of the ways that the Church undertook to make its authority felt was in the development of a systematic body of Canon Law or Church Law. And this Canon Law would in fact constitute the foundation of all subsequent civil and criminal law in Western Europe.[29]

The Catholic Church was aided in this task by the fortuitous rediscovery in Italy in the 11th century of the Digest, a compendium of fifty books on Roman Law that the Emperor Justinian had compiled in the year 533 A.D. In seeking to establish a legal system for Church law, Catholic jurists made use not only of the newly rediscovered Roman law but also made important contributions of their own using theology, philosophy, and natural law theory. They thus provided a solid, theological, rational, and intellectual basis for the law and, in doing so, forged the basis of the great western legal tradition.[30]

An example of the Catholic Church's contribution can be seen in the work of St. Anselm of Canterbury. In the late 11th century, he developed a theology of the Redemption, showing that since original sin has disturbed the moral order of the universe, atonement had to be made to set things right and satisfy the demands of Justice. He thus provided a reasoned argument for the atoning death of Christ. Subsequent to St. Anselm, the criminal law that developed in Western Europe was profoundly influenced by his doctrine of atonement. To violate the law was to offend justice and to upset the moral order. The offense had to be punished if the moral order was to be set right. And it was crucial that the nature and severity of the punishment fit the crime. This principle was extended to such other areas as the law of contracts (breach of contract required

---

29   Harold J. Berman, *Law and Revolution* (Cambridge: Harvard University Press, 1985).
30   Berman, *Law and Revolution*.

just compensation), the law of torts (a just amount of damages had to be paid to compensate the injury), property rights (restitution must be made to the person whose property rights had been violated), etc.

The concept of the Rule of Law flowed necessarily from these principles. Any violation of the law by anyone, no matter who, constituted a breach of the moral order, and justice demanded that it be set right. Hence the law applied to everyone, no matter what his status.

The development of the rule of law in the western legal tradition is also a result of another important Christian insight. In the Gospel of St. John, Christ says to Pilate: "You would have no authority over me unless it had been given you from above."[31] And in his Epistle to the Romans, St. Paul says, "Let every person be subject to the governing authorities. For there is no authority except from God, and those that exist have been instituted by God."[32] From these passages, the Church understood that the sovereign receives his authority from God and that he is answerable to God for how he governs. He is thus answerable to a higher law and must respect the natural law and human rights. In the year 1215 A.D., for example, the Archbishop of Canterbury, Stephen Langton, led the barons of England to confront King John and forced him to sign the Magna Carta, which is considered a crucial document in the history of the development of the rule of law. [33]

In most medieval political regimes it was understood that political authority devolved from God to the people who confirmed the choice of the sovereign and supported him as long as their rights were respected. After the break-up of Christendom in the 16th century, Europe witnessed a period of rule by absolute monarchs, followed by the modern period of representative democracies. But in all three cases it was understood that the government's authority derives ultimately from God, and that the sovereign must respect natural law and human rights.

The preamble to the Declaration of Independence of the United States in the 18th century makes this abundantly clear:

> When in the Course of human events it becomes necessary for one people to dissolve the political bands which have connected them with another and to assume among the powers of the earth, **the separate and equal station to which the Laws of Nature and of Nature's God entitle them,** a decent respect to the opinions of mankind requires that they should declare the causes which impel them to the separation.

---

31   Jn. 19:11, (Revised Standard Version: Second Catholic Edition).
32   Rom. 13:1, (Revised Standard Version: Second Catholic Edition).
33   "Magna Carta and Human Rights," *Rule of Law Education Centre*, July 13, 2022, https://www.ruleoflaw.org.au/magna-carta-and-human-rights/#:~:text=The%20Magna%20Carta%20established%20the%20rule%20of%20law,to%20justice%20and%20the%20protection%20of%20human%20rights.

> We hold these truths to be self-evident, **that all men are created**
> **equal, that they are endowed by their Creator with certain unalienable**
> **Rights, that among these are Life, Liberty and the pursuit of Happiness.**

Basing itself on the fact that ultimate authority comes from God, the Christian Tradition holds that there are necessary moral constraints on the content of law, and any law that does not respect natural law and human rights is not a true law, at all and there is no obligation to obey it.[34]

Expressive Individualism abandoned the principle that all governmental authority derives ultimately from God and has also accordingly abandoned the principle that governments must respect the natural law. They have replaced this principle with a theory called legal positivism, which itself has evolved into what is known as legal realism. This theory contends that law is socially constructed. It consists of legislation and case law and is independent of any natural law. Legislation is considered valid if it has been enacted according to law and cannot be rendered invalid by any appeal to natural law.[35] Since this approach leaves open the possibility of the exercise of arbitrary power by the government, most liberal democracies have created declarations of human rights and imbedded them in their constitutions. So, laws may be challenged if they violate one of the rights protected by the constitution, but any appeal to natural law or human rights not protected by the constitution is considered out of bounds and will fail.

As we saw above, this has led to a proliferation of supposedly human rights while consigning some traditional and fundamental human rights, such as freedom of conscience, to second-class status. Furthermore, once God is no longer considered the source of political authority, Expressive Individualism has trouble grounding the rights and freedoms that it wishes to protect. For example, the first sentence of the preamble of the United Nations' Universal Declaration of Human Rights reads as follows: "Whereas recognition of the inherent dignity and of the equal and inalienable rights of all members of the human family is the foundation of freedom, justice, and peace in the world." The declaration refers to the inherent dignity and inalienable rights of each person, but it does not mention how that dignity and those rights are grounded. Jacques Maritain, one of the drafters of the Declaration, said that the only way to reach agreement had been to set aside all speculative notions about the world, man, and knowledge, and concentrate on common practical notions upon which the member states could agree.[36]

---

34 *Catechism of the Catholic Church*, 1959; Saint Augustine, *De Libero Arbitrio*, I, 5.
35 John Lawrence Hill, *After the Natural Law* (San Francisco: Ignatius Press, 2016), 239-40.
36 William Sweet, "Jacques Maritain," in *Stanford Encyclopedia of Philosophy* (Stanford University: Summer 2022), https://plato.stanford.edu/entries/maritain/.

Separation of Church and State

Another principle that is vital to the economic prosperity of a nation is the principle of the separation of Church and State. We take this principle for granted. However, before the advent of Christianity, the idea of separate religious and political orders was unknown. People worshipped the gods of the particular state in which they lived. Religion was usually no more than a department of the state. In some cases, however, it was the religious authorities who held political power.

The Christian insight into the distinction between the secular and the spiritual is founded on the words of Jesus: "Render to Caesar the things that are Caesar's, and to God the things that are God's"[37] With this phrase, Christ effected the greatest revolution in political theory that the world has ever witnessed. It was this distinction between Church and State that would eventually take hold in Western Europe and which would ultimately lead to the religious tolerance that we witness today. However, it would take many centuries before the consequences of this message would be implanted in Western civilization.[38] Christ's words implied the existence of two distinct areas of human life and activity. Hence a theory of two powers came to form the basis of Christian thought and teaching from the earliest times.

Christianity teaches that the Church and the state are differentiated from each other by their nature and by their aims. The Church is of the supernatural order, and its aim is supernatural: the salvation of souls. The state belongs to the natural order, and its purpose is the temporal common good of civil society, which means that the state should seek to create and foster those social conditions that allow people, either as groups or as individuals, to reach their fulfillment more fully and more easily. In essence, the state should adopt laws and policies in accordance with the natural law and make it easy for men to pursue their own end. It should promote peace, order, justice, freedom, culture, the rule of law, respect for human rights, etc.[39]

Why is this separation of Church and state important? History teaches us that when there is no such separation, the human rights and especially the religious freedom of the members of society are almost always violated. When Church and State are one, refusal to follow the official religion of the state is considered an attack upon the state itself. So those belonging to a minority religion will frequently be persecuted, or even deported or killed. Those who are lax in the fulfillment of their religious duties will often be punished. Religion will regularly be used by the government to further its political agenda, thereby

---

37   Mk. 12:17 (Revised Standard Version: Second Catholic Edition).
38   Walter Ullman, *Medieval Political Thought* (City of Westminster: Penguin Books, 1965).
39   Catechism of the Catholic Church, 2104-2109, 2244-2246, 2419-2425.

discrediting religion and making people cynical about it. And if it is the religious authorities who gain political power, they will frequently pursue a religious agenda to the detriment of the economic prosperity of the nation.

A case in point is premodern China, which saw early developments of capitalism, science, and technology. However, all three major systems of thought in premodern China (Confucianism, Daoism or Taoism, and Buddhism) viewed these developments as unessential to man's well-being, and so the attempts to develop capitalism, science, and technology were not encouraged by the governments of the day at the insistence of religious leaders.[40] So, the separation of church and state is another great achievement of Western Civilization that we owe to Christianity. In Expressive Individualism, however, this notion of the separation of church and state has been detached from its Christian roots and its meaning radically altered.

Traditionally, it was understood that since men live in society, the Church has to set out moral guidelines and teach the implications of the Gospel to social and political life in light of the truth about man. In this way, the Church contributes to the human progress of society. The Church as an institution should not be directly involved in political life, but it was understood that its members, on their own initiative and responsibility, should become involved and make a positive contribution to society by proposing the Church's social teaching as a basis for the state's laws.

Also, religious freedom was understood to mean the freedom of a person to live according to his religious beliefs, provided that those beliefs do not violate public order. Expressive Individualism has shrunk the definition of religious freedom to freedom of worship. By this, it means that everyone is free to attend the church, synagogue, mosque, or temple of his choice or not to attend any religious service. But the freedom to lead a life according to on one's beliefs stops when those beliefs come into conflict with the personal autonomy of others, as understood by Expressive Individualism. And in Expressive Individualism the separation of Church and state has been radicalized to the point where any public expression or display of religion is forbidden in the U.S., and any proposal that is seen as religiously based is considered illegitimate for discussion in the public sphere. A Christian legislator is supposed to keep his religiously based ideas to himself. It is normal that the specific dictates of a given religion should not form the basis of laws. There should be no law compelling citizens to attend religious services or requiring them to abstain from meat on Fridays or to go on a pilgrimage to Mecca once in their lifetime. But the Church's teachings that are based on natural law should not be considered out of bounds. For example, its teaching on the dignity of the human person, on the value of life from conception to natural death, on marriage, on justice, on human rights,

---

40   Needham, *Science and Civilization in China, Vol. 1.*

etc. are based on natural law and are shared by many people of different religions or no religion.

Every legislator has personal beliefs on how society should be run, and he seeks to implement those ideas. It is irrational to exclude certain ideas from the discussion because it is believed that their source is religious. Yet, this is what has happened. Ideas that do not conform to Expressive Individualism are considered unworthy of receiving a hearing.

Free Market Economies

The global income per person per day in the first century A.D. was $2.00 as measured in 2011 American Dollars. A thousand years later it was still $2.00 per day. This does not mean that no economic growth took place over that long period. There was some growth, but it was minimal, local, and could not be sustained because of droughts, wars, etc. Whatever growth there was inevitably petered out.

Much the same can be said about the next seven hundred years. Until the early 18th century, most people still lived in poverty and squalor. Over those seven hundred years, average global income had risen by only 40% to $2.80. It was uneven, of course, and so some regions had a higher average income than others. But starting in the 18th century, an economic miracle took place. Beginning in England and Holland and quickly spreading to the rest of Western Europe and North America, industrialization and free market economics caused GDP to rise dramatically, lifting those populations out of poverty. And this economic miracle has not ceased to this day and has little by little spread to the rest of the world. The 20th century witnessed great increases in life expectancy, gross domestic product, and literacy, as well as dramatic falls in infant mortality, extreme poverty, and malnutrition.[41]

Expressive Individualism would maintain that we were only able to escape from indigence and poverty by casting off the influence of religion. However, if we examine the economic miracle more closely, we will see that without certain insights that had been imbedded in the culture by Christianity, free market economics, and the industrial revolution could never have happened. And this is why the miracle originated in Christian Europe and North America rather than somewhere else.

By free market economics, we simply mean the purchase and sale of goods through free enterprise, via peaceful social cooperation without undue

41   "World GDP over the last two millennia", Our World in Data, July 6, 2023, https://www.visualcapitalist.com/2000-years-economic-history-one-chart/; https://ourworldindata.org/grapher/world-gdp-over-the-last-two-millennia?time=1..latest.

interference by government. As it develops over time, free market economics becomes a system whereby private companies engage in commercial transactions within a relatively unregulated market and produce goods or services using a hired work force with an anticipation of profit.

Historians still disagree about the precise causes of the industrial revolution. But it is clear that in order for it to have happened, some key factors had to be in place. Some of these we have seen previously:

- **The rule of law and the security of private property rights.** Industrialization requires investment. If contracts cannot be enforced by the courts and if property rights are not secure, there will be no investment.
- **Limited Government.** If the sovereign can exercise arbitrary power and seize whatever he likes, then once again people will not invest in factories or other businesses. And if the government takes on a major role in the economy, one ends up with state-controlled planned economies, which have consistently proven to be disastrous.
- **The conviction that progress is possible and that mankind is called to master nature.** Innovation was crucial to the industrial revolution, and it was this insight from Christianity that encouraged innovation.
- **Freedom and Individual Human Rights.** Without the freedom to innovate and the right to engage in trade for oneself, industrialization would not have happened.
- **The Spirit of Rational Inquiry.** Free market economics and capitalism are pursued in a highly rational way as a science. As we saw above, it was Christianity that gifted this spirit of rational inquiry to western civilization.
- **The importance of productivity and the value of work.** In 1905, the German sociologist Max Weber published his famous work, *The Protestant Ethic and the Spirit of Capitalism*. In it, he attributes the rise of capitalism to the Protestant work ethic and its understanding of work as a calling from God. Although parts of his thesis have been discredited by other scholars over the years, some of the points that he made are still valid. Even prior to the 16th century Reformation, the Catholic Church had taught that all work, including manual work, was valuable in the eyes of God, since God himself, in the person of Christ, had worked for 30 years as a craftsman in Nazareth. Declaring all work noble meant that not only agriculture but also trade, business, investing, etc. were noble callings.

Many factors contributed to the economic miracle. But it is safe to say that without the six factors set out above, it could never have taken place. And as we saw earlier in this chapter, all of those factors are due to Christianity. As with the other achievements noted in this chapter, Christianity's teaching on natural law did seek to impose strict ethical limits on the way capitalism was carried out. The Church has always condemned unbridled capitalism, which is motivated by greed and selfishness. It sees the exploitation of others as sinful. And it sees a consumerist mentality as degrading to the human person. In dealing with capitalism, the Catholic Church puts an emphasis on the notion of solidarity. By this it does not mean some vague sentiment of compassion for our suffering brothers, but rather the firm resolve to persevere in working for the common good in spite of the personal sacrifice it calls for. It points out the need to build structures and systems that will foster justice and solidarity for the good of all. The natural law should be used to guide economic development. If this happens, capitalism will be at the service of the whole person and all people.[42] Even though Christianity's contribution was crucial to the emergence of industrialization and free market economics, capitalism has evolved on its own and often does not abide by the ethical limits that flow from natural law.

Conclusion

In the conclusion of his book, *The Victory of Reason*, Rodney Stark says the following:

> Christianity created Western Civilization. Had the followers of Jesus remained an obscure Jewish sect, most of you would not have learned to read and the rest of you would be reading from hand copied scrolls. Without a theology committed to reason, progress and moral equality, today the entire world would be about where non-European societies were in say, 1800. A world with many astrologers and alchemists, but no scientists. A world of despots, lacking universities, banks, factories, eyeglasses, chimneys and pianos. A world where most infants do not live to the age of five and many women die in childbirth—a world truly living in dark ages.[43]

The scientific, technical, and commercial knowledge of the West has now spread around the globe. And in the West, as we have seen, Expressive Individualism seeks to appropriate these advances for itself while decoupling them from their grounding in Christian teaching and natural law. The question is, up to what point can these advances be sustained without that foundation? That will be the subject of our next chapter.

---

42 Andrew Swafford, "What Does the Church Say about Capitalism?," Ascension Press, June 21, 2018. https://media.ascensionpress.com/2018/06/21/what-does-the-church-say-about-capitalism/.

43 Rodney Stark, *The Victory of Reason* (New York: Random House, 2005), 233.

Chapter 6

Expressive Individualism and the Idea of Justice[1]

"Man has always lost his way; but modern man has lost his address."[2]
—G.K. Chesterton, *What's Wrong With the World*

As we saw in Chapter 2, one of the main themes of Expressive Individualism is liberty or personal autonomy. It considers autonomy to be an essential characteristic of personhood to the point that one's dignity lies in being an autonomous human being who can choose his own values and his own way of life. This is at times referred to as the imperial self, the sovereign individual, or the autonomous self.

This autonomy means self-definition: each individual decides his own values, his own meaning of life and neither the state nor anyone else should interfere with his right to pursue that vision and lead the life he chooses. The state should uphold and enforce the Do No Harm Principle; but apart from that it should remain neutral and refrain from imposing or endorsing any particular conception of the good life or of what gives value to life. A state violates the equal respect, equal concern, self-respect, dignity or other good that it owes its citizens if it upholds a specific version of the good that subverts an individual's autonomous choices.

Expressive Individualism justifies this position in several ways. Since it considers morality to be relative and holds that there are no universal moral truths apart from the Do No Harm principle, the state should not impose any moral beliefs on its citizens. Since controversial moral issues divide citizens and cause civil discontent, the state should remove those issues from the political process for the sake of keeping the peace, unless the Do No Harm principle comes into play. Also, for the sake of competition. The state's neutrality will allow the best of competing ideas to emerge and win out. Thus, each one should adopt his or her own values, his or her own truth, and should respect the choice of values that others adopt. As long as living out your values doesn't harm anyone else, you are free to do whatever you like, and no one should

---

1   John Safranek, *The Myth of Liberalism* (Washington: The Catholic University of America Press, 2015). The discussion in the first half of this chapter is based on the given citation.

2   G.K. Chesterton, *What's Wrong with the World* (New York: Dodd, Mead and Company, 1910), Part I, Chapter IX.

judge your conduct. All choices are equally valid so long as they respect the Do No Harm Principle.

This permits many different kinds of lifestyles (common-law unions, divorced and remarried couples, same-sex couples, multiple partners, transgendered individuals, etc.). It allows those who wish to end their lives to do so. It allows free choice on the questions of contraception and abortion. In short, it empowers everyone and so enriches society.

It multiplies the range of available options without obliging anyone to adopt any particular option, and this grants a greater degree of freedom to everyone, leading to more happiness. The problem with all this is that, in practice, the state cannot remain neutral. It is always obliged to impose some notion of the good.

First of all, it has to outlaw murder, theft, rape, assault, terrorism, and other clearly criminal acts. By doing so, the state is imposing a notion of the good on society. In these cases, the notion of the good is the Do No Harm Principle. However, every law that the state enacts embodies a view of the good. Laws imposing construction standards, zoning by-laws, laws that allow expropriation, laws imposing monogamy, etc. The state is effectively infringing the autonomy of many people whenever it enacts any law.

A person's idea of the good may be to build his own house without regard to the building code. Or to set up a business in a residential area. Or to keep his house when the state wants to expropriate it to build a highway. Or to be married to more than one woman. If the law prohibits these actions, it is infringing on his autonomy.

The state can't even be neutral on a simple issue like raising the minimum wage. By raising it, the state is infringing on the autonomy of employers whose values and whose view of life preclude the state forcing them to pay their employees more. Indeed, whenever there is a clash of interests or rights claims autonomy can't be used to solve the issue, because any decision will negatively affect the autonomy of one of the parties. The decision needs to be based on another principle, on a concept of the good, which means on a notion of justice, which means it has to be based on a concept of objective ethics or morality that goes to the very heart of the human person and his purpose. Those who embrace Expressive Individualism refuse to admit this.

This is one inherent contradiction that lies at the heart of Expressive Individualism. It seeks to base itself on autonomy, but is frequently forced to limit autonomy. And it seeks some way to do this without violating autonomy. In order to function, Expressive Individualism must be bound to a concept of the good and morality. But it contradicts its own fundamental principles by being so bound. When it is pointed out that autonomy can't be used to settle competing interests or rights claims

Expressive Individualism falls back on other principles to decide the issue. Some of these include:

- Equality
- Human rights
- Do No Harm
- Utilitarianism
- Privacy
- Liberty
- Dignity

However, as we shall see, all these principles ultimately run into the same problem as the autonomy principle. We can use ten examples to illustrate this:

1. A baker is happy to serve his gay customers. However, when one wishes to commission him to prepare a cake to celebrate his same-sex wedding, the baker refuses, since in conscience he believes that marriage must be between a man and a woman, and his conscience does not allow him to use his artistic abilities to create a cake to celebrate a same-sex wedding. The baker believes he has the right to refuse to bake the cake, and his customer believes that he has a right to demand it.

2. A doctor who is not a religious believer refuses to perform euthanasia or even to refer a patient to another doctor who will, since in that way he would be collaborating in an act that violates the Hippocratic oath that he took and which his conscience judges to be immoral. This results in a clash between the doctor's worldview and that of the person who desires to end his life.

3. A female athlete is denied a gold medal in an athletic competition because she is defeated by a stronger biological male athlete who identifies as a female and claims the right to participate as a woman. Once again, there is a clash of rights claims.

4. A woman wants some privacy from men in the women's locker room. She objects to the presence there of a biological male who identifies as a female. The biological male considers that he has a right to use the locker room since he identifies as a woman.

5. Invoking their rights to exercise parental authority, the parents of a minor want to pull him out of a sex-ed class whose content they disagree with. The school insists that it has the right to oblige the minor to attend since the class will impart something important for the child's education. Or the parents of a minor who is experiencing gender dysphoria want him to undergo psychological counselling, whereas the school doctor insists that the mental health of the boy requires him to rather begin taking puberty blockers. Or the parents of a minor who is experiencing same-sex attraction want him to

undergo conversion therapy, but the school's social worker insists
that this would violate the boy's rights.

6. A Chinese student complains that he has not been admitted into a
    certain prestigious university because a set number of places have
    been reserved for other racial minorities, even though most of those
    students are not as qualified academically as the Chinese student.
    The university justifies itself by saying that it is simply righting
    an historic wrong by admitting the students from other racial
    minorities.

7. A gay student in a Catholic school claims the right to bring his
    boyfriend to the prom, but the school is not allowing this since it
    violates Catholic moral teaching.

8. A Catholic adoption agency wants to place orphans only in families
    where there is an opposite sex husband and wife present and not
    with same-sex couples. The government insists that it must also
    place orphans with same-sex couples.

9. A Christian nurse does not want to help in surgical abortion
    procedures, since she considers abortion to be the unjust taking of
    the life of an innocent and defenseless child. The hospital insists
    that all nurses must take part in these procedures when called
    upon to do so.

10 A pro-life speaker is invited to deliver an address on campus. A large
    group of abortion rights activists interrupt the speaker and render it
    impossible for him to deliver his speech. The pro-abortion activists
    claim that the address is a form of hate speech and so should not be
    allowed to proceed.

The seven principles mentioned above cannot succeed in solving the clash
of rights in these ten cases, because each of these principles is no more than a
different way of referring to autonomy. We will examine them one at a time.

Equality[3]

At first glance, equality seems to be a more compelling principle than autonomy.
Autonomy says I have a right to do X because I want to. This can look egocentric
and arbitrary. Equality says I have a right to do X because others in my same
situation have also been granted this right.

In law, the principle of equality is usually referred to as substantive equal
protection. This means that everyone's choices and acts will be treated equally
by the law and before the courts. More specifically, it means that two relevantly
similar persons who are in relevantly similar situations will be treated equally.

---

3   Safranek, "Equality and Freedom" in *The Myth of Liberalism*.

The qualifier *relevantly* is necessary. An imprisoned felon is not in a relevantly similar situation to one who is not imprisoned and may not demand certain rights that the person who is not imprisoned can demand. A drunk driver cannot demand equal treatment to one who drives prudently. A businessman who acts fraudulently will not be treated in the same way as an honest businessman, etc. In each case, though, what is required is a standard by which to ascertain whether the two persons are in a relevantly similar situation. And the principle of equality as such cannot generate that standard. That standard can only be generated by a theory of justice and an underlying concept of the moral good. In the third example above, the female athlete wants to be treated as equal to other female athletes and so compete against them. The biological male who self-identifies as female wants to be treated as equal to other females. The principle of equality can't be applied until it is established whether the two are relevantly equal. And that cannot be decided by the principle of equality, but only by other criteria.

Equality can mean many different things: equality of outcome or opportunity; equality based on need, merit, or effort. Imagine the case of a father who, in his will, leaves his fortune to his three sons in equal parts. The older son claims that he should receive more because he worked with his father for years and contributed to the father's amassing of the fortune. The second son has a disability and so claims that he should receive a greater share because he is most in need. The youngest son claims that his two older brothers have spent many more years than him benefiting from their father's wealth, and so he should receive a greater share to make up for this. The father has based his legacy on one understanding of justice. Each of his sons is appealing to a different theory of justice. It is obvious that the principle of equality means nothing until the question of the standard to be used in this case is settled.[4] As Peter Westen has said in the Harvard Law Review, "Equality is an empty vessel with no substantive content of its own. Without moral standards, it remains meaningless, a formula that can say nothing about how we should act."[5] In other words, by itself, the principle of equality, like the principle of autonomy, cannot resolve competing interests or rights claims. Each one needs a theory of justice and a concept of the moral good in order to be applied. In this sense, equality and autonomy come down to the same thing.

4   Safranek, *The Myth of Liberalism*, 52-54. This example is taken from the given citation.
5   Peter Westen, "The Empty Idea of Equality," *Harvard Law Review* 95, no. 3 (1982): 537-596.

Human Rights[6]

In Expressive Individualism each person has a human right to equality before the law and to life, liberty, and the pursuit of happiness. Included in these last two categories is the human right to pursue one's own life project in the measure that it does not harm others. Hence, a person can claim that he has a human right to do anything that is needed to pursue his life project. It should be immediately obvious that this recourse to human rights by Expressive Individualism will fail on the same grounds as autonomy. If two persons justify their behaviour by claiming that they have a human right to act in that way, it is obvious that the clash can't be solved by recourse to human rights doctrine itself. Once again, the clash can only be solved by a theory of justice and of the moral good. In deciding these cases, the courts will sometimes refer to a right as a fundamental right and prioritize it over the opposing rights claim. But in order to know which rights are fundamental, one once again requires a concept of justice, of the good, and of natural law.

There can be a clash of rights claims because no human right is absolute, even those that we might consider the most fundamental, even the right to life itself. If I enter a school with a gun and begin shooting at students, I forfeit my right to life, and a security guard will be justified in killing me. The right to practice my faith (freedom of religion) is not absolute either. If my religion requires me to sacrifice my firstborn child to my gods, I will be prohibited by law from practicing that aspect of it. In order to judge between two persons who both claim that they have a human right to act in a certain way, the court must use the criteria of justice to decide. In fact, every law that sets out a right can also be expressed in terms of justice without loss of meaning. Up until the 18th century, societies were able to function in a just way without reference to individual rights. In order to defend himself in court against a challenge, someone who claimed the freedom to act in certain way had to prove that his claim was justified because it was in accordance with justice. He did not need to have recourse to human rights doctrine.[7] Therefore, human rights doctrine as such cannot solve the ten cases above any better than the principles of equality or autonomy can. An underlying concept of justice is necessary. And, as we have said, justice relies on a concept of the good and ultimately of natural law. As we will briefly show, none of the other principles can successfully be used to judge between competing interests or rights claims.

---

6   Safranek, "Rights and Freedom" in *The Myth of Liberalism.*
7   Safranek, *The Myth of Liberalism,* 97-98.

Do No Harm

The principle states that one has the right to live out one's concept of the good life, provided he does not harm anyone else. And in Expressive Individualism, harm includes preventing someone else from living out his values, engaging in his lifestyle, and leading the life of his choice. When there is a clash of interests, each side claiming that the actions of the other are harming him, Expressive Individualism must necessarily prioritize some interests over others. And that can only be based on one's view of the good. If harm includes being unable to pursue the life of one's choice, then the harm principle cannot be used to settle competing claims. There is no real distinction between the Do No Harm principle and autonomy.

Utilitarianism[8]

The original utilitarian principle stated that decisions should be made in order to maximize the pleasure or happiness of the greatest number of people. Expressive Individualism has substituted the notion of preferences for pleasure or happiness. So in Expressive Individualism, decisions should be made in order to satisfy or maximize the preferences of the greatest number of people, including, of course, the preferences of minorities. However, the preferences of different societal groups will inevitably clash, and hence the autonomy of some people will simply have to be curtailed in order to favour the greater autonomy of the many. But curtailing the autonomy of some people violates Expressive Individualism. In addition, what if the preferences of the many are unjust? The preferences of the many may be to impose an unjust burden on a minority sector of the population. None of our principles are adequate to dealing with this, not even the Do No Harm principle, since to deny the majority the right to pursue their preferences would be to harm them. Once again, only a recourse to justice can solve this problem.

Privacy

The courts have defined privacy as the right to make personal decisions and act on them free from state interference. This is essentially no different from autonomy.

---

8   Safranek, "Liberalism and Utilitarianism" in *The Myth of Liberalism.*

Liberty

The court has defined liberty as self-determination: the ability independently to define one's identity, one's concept of the good, and the determination of one's life plan. Again, this is autonomy under another name.

Dignity

For the Expressive Individualist, one's dignity resides in being, to some important degree, a person of one's own creating, making, or choosing to be a self-constituted, unique, individual person. This clearly comes down to autonomy.

It should be clear by now that none of these principles can be used to solve the ten cases and many others, because a decision in favour of one party will negatively impact the autonomy of the other. The only way to solve issues like these is to base one's decision on a concept of the good, which implies a theory of Justice and an objective moral law.

This is in fact fairly self-evident. Anyone who gives any serious thought to this question will realize that in order to resolve competing rights claims, there is need for a theory of justice that goes beyond autonomy and the other principles mentioned above. Since those who hold to Expressive Individualism do not want to admit the need for a theory of morality in judging these cases, they have recourse to another stratagem in the form of what is referred to as **Public Reason** or the **Reasonable Consensus.**

This theory, as we saw in Chapter 2, maintains that as a society evolves, a common consensus on moral issues forms that considers any conduct that harms others to be immoral. This consensus changes over time as society becomes more enlightened, and when this happens, the laws naturally adopt the new criteria. The abolition of slavery and the prohibition of interracial marriage are examples. This reasonable consensus or public reason becomes the foundation for a society's laws. It is seen as a standard for assessing customs, laws, institutions, and the behavior of individual citizens and public officials. It becomes the only external criteria of morality for citizens. As Stephen Macedo, one of the leading liberal thinkers, has stated:

> In order to justify our political arrangements with good reasons, we assume we can be true to something beyond mere likes and dislikes, personal will and arbitrary preference: to reasons that count as reasons for others and not only for ourselves, to reasons that can be publicly stated and knit into a critically defensible and widely accessible moral framework.[9]

9   Stephen Macedo, *Liberal Virtues* (Oxford: Clarendon Press, 1990), 41.

On the one hand, Expressive Individualism rejects the objectivity of the moral law in the name of autonomy but, on the other hand, establishes an objective framework of ethics, calling it Public Reason or the Reasonable Consensus. Expressive Individualism considers this ethical framework to be in line with reason, and so every reasonable person should subscribe to it. Indeed, it is incumbent upon every citizen to accept it since we should all act rationally and reasonably. And, as we shall see in chapter 7, public reason severely curtails the freedom and autonomy of those who do not subscribe to it.

Now, in theory, the content of Public Reason or the Reasonable Consensus should indeed reflect a consensus of the general public on these issues. The very notion of consensus requires that the moral or political rules that regulate our common life be, in some sense, justifiable or acceptable to all or at least most of those persons over whom the rules purport to have authority. However, anyone who has given even passing attention to the political and cultural situation in the U.S. over the past 25 years knows that the reality is somewhat different. There is simply no consensus but rather a polarized country engaged in a culture war.

Those who devise and disseminate Expressive Individualism consider themselves to be Progressives. They hold that history moves according to a rational, discernible purpose, specifically in the direction of a gradual but irreversible amelioration of the human condition, understood especially as an ever-increasing equality.[10]

These liberal thinkers, academics, jurists, political theorists, journalists, billionaires, influential opinion makers, etc. see themselves as uniquely qualified to guide this progress and so to formulate the best possible worldview—one that will benefit all mankind. They hold that their natural superiority entitles them to rule. They do not trust the majority to arrive at a reasonable consensus. They believe that it is they who must assume the responsibility for deciding what is reasonable, what is best for the general population. The reasonable consensus is the one that they arrive at.[11]

In their minds, governance requires an elite class, who possess a certain kind of historical intelligence and insight,[12] people with a certain moral, intellectual, and cultural superiority, which is demonstrated by their status and their solicitude for identity groups that have been historically oppressed. With

---

10   Carson Holloway "The Sources of Liberal Intolerance," *Public Discourse*, September 17, 2010, https://www.thepublicdiscourse.com/2010/09/1644/.

11   Safranek, *The Myth of Liberalism*, 159.

12   Bradley C.S. Watson, "Darwin's Constitution," *National Review*, May 17, 2010, https://www.nationalreview.com/magazine/2010/05/17/darwins-constitution/.

their intelligence and expertise they will create a vast state mechanism that will ensure growth by means of progressive education, the administrative state, and redistribution of capital.[13]

Progressives see themselves as creating a better world and as entitled to impose their values, even at great cost to those who disagree with them, in order to achieve that goal.[14] The Reasonable Consensus that they put forth is not to be subject to debate. It is, quite simply, the most reasonable worldview possible, since it is based on reason. If the majority fails to agree, then the majority is not just in error, but has no legitimacy as a source of political authority.[15] Progressives propose a deal. They say something akin to,

> Since we know best what is good for you, you agree to leave political power in our hands, and we will ensure that there is freedom, peace, justice, economic growth, and equality as a result of the Reasonable Consensus that we will implement. In our wisdom, we will take care of settling any disagreements that arise over conflicting rights claims. We will also give you hedonism: a high standard of living, free sex, access to unlimited entertainment, to the latest technologies and to consumer goods, and the right to do and be whatever you wish.

So what is the content of Public Reason or the Reasonable Consensus? What criteria does it provide that would allow the legislators and the courts to resolve the clashing rights claims set out above?

These Progressives consider that Western Civilization has utterly failed to deliver a world of equality, peace and fraternity. The 20th Century, which should have ushered in a world of this type was, on the contrary, marked by wars and genocides. Furthermore, Western Civilization, as they see it, is inherently immoral, thoroughly permeated by white privilege,[16] homophobia,[17]

---

13   J. Michael Hogan, *Rhetoric and Reform in the Progressive Era* (East Lansing: Michigan State University Press, 2003); James Kalb, *The Tyranny of Liberalism,* (Wilmington: ISI Books, 2008), 50.

14   Margaret Somerville, "It Didn't Happen Overnight," *Mercatornet,* June 7, 2016, https://web.archive.org/web/20230529162951/https://mercatornet.com/it-didnt-happen-overnight/20805/.

15   Nathanael Blake, "The Dual Legitimation Crisis: Elitism, Populism, and Political Power," *Public Discourse,* April 24, 2018, https://www.thepublicdiscourse.com/2018/04/21326/; Patrick J. Deneen, *Why Liberalism Failed* (New Haven: Yale University Press, 2018), 156-161.

16   Jon Greenberg, "10 Examples That Prove White Privilege Exists in Every Aspect Imaginable," *Yes! Magazine,* July 24, 2017, https://www.yesmagazine.org/social-justice/2017/07/24/10-examples-that-prove-white-privilege-exists-in-every-aspect-imaginable/.

17   Sejal Singh and Laura E. Durso, "Widespread Discrimination Continues to Shape LGBT People's Lives in Both Subtle and Significant Ways," Center for American Progress, May 2, 2017, https://www.americanprogress.org/issues/lgbtq-rights/news/2017/05/02/429529/widespread-discrimination-continues-shape-lgbt-peoples-lives-subtle-significant-ways/.

transphobia,[18] misogyny,[19] sexism,[20] heteronormativity, Islamophobia[21], systemic racism[22], religious superstition, gross inequalities, etc. One analyst, who experienced this first hand at Berkeley, had this to say about the cohort of professors and administrators there:

> Their principal thesis is marked by its incredible want of nuance: American (and or Western) culture, history, and systems of government are inherently and irreparably evil.
>
> This evil is ubiquitous and inextricable, and it manifests in the world most pronouncedly in patriarchal tyranny, homophobia, racism, and white supremacy. The evidence of such evils need not be clear or even present, but is so unquestionably foundational to our society, that one need only place the word "systemic" in front of any word to silence requests for supporting data. Those who fail to accept the theory on faith are treated as infidels, socially ostracized at best, and totally cast out of their institution at worst.
>
> These evils corrupt the foundations of any structure where they are perceived to be present. The process of rooting them out, then, necessitates the destruction of the structure in its entirety. The assertion that the United States itself, its origins, its founding documents, its historic figures, global influence, and its rule of law are all infected by this pernicious virus, justifies virtually every assault against it.[23]

They believe that Western Civilization must be replaced by a new civilization, a Brave New World, a secular utopia where there will be none of these things but rather justice, peace, equality, and happiness. They understand, of course, that there will never be a perfect society. But they do believe in unlimited progress.[24]

18   Jeremy W. Peters, "Why Transgender Girls Are Suddenly the G.O.P.'s Culture-War Focus," *New York Times*, March 29, 2021, https://www.nytimes.com/2021/03/29/us/politics/transgender-girls-sports.html.

19   Kalpana Srivastava, "Misogyny, Feminism, and Sexual Harassment," *Industrial Psychology Journal* 26, no. 2 (2017): 111–113. https://www.ncbi.nlm.nih.gov/pmc/articles/PMC6058438/.

20   Jim Tankersley, "How Sexism Follows Women From the Cradle to the Workplace," *The New York Times*, August 19, 2018, https://www.nytimes.com/2018/08/19/business/sexism-women-birthplace-workplace.html.

21   Aslam Abdullah, "Sources of Islamophobia," *Islamicity*, March 22, 2019, https://www.islamicity.org/18988/sources-of-islamophobia/.

22   Nicholas Lemann, "Is Capitalism Racist? A scholar depicts white supremacy as the economic engine of American history," *The New Yorker Magazine*, May 18, 2020, https://www.newyorker.com/magazine/2020/05/25/is-capitalism-racist.

23   Madison Breshears, "Wake Up: Our Cultural Crisis is A Graduate of the American University," *Medium*, July 10, 2020, https://medium.com/@mbreshears/wake-up-our-cultural-crisis-is-a-graduate-of-the-american-university-9bec944ddf99.

24   Melanie Phillips, *The World Turned Upside Down: The Global Battle Over God, Truth, and Power* (New York: Encounter Books, 2010), 257-9, 282-3; Kalb, *The Tyranny of Liberalism*, 25; Margaret Somerville, *Bird on an Ethics Wire: Battles about Values in the Culture Wars*; (Montreal: McGill-Queen's University Press, 2015), 6.

For example, some of the lyrics of John Lennon's song "Imagine" reflect this desire for a new civilization. In that song, he envisions a world free from divisions and conflicts. The lyrics suggest imagining a world without Heaven or Hell, without countries, or religions—where people live peacefully and focus on the present. It also envisions a world without possessions, greed, or hunger, where humanity lives in harmony and shares resources. Lennon acknowledges that this vision may seem idealistic, but he expresses hope that others will join in working towards this unified, peaceful world.

In 1987, Jesse Jackson led a protest of around 500 students at Stanford University chanting "Hey hey, ho ho, Western Civ has got to go."[25] They were ostensibly protesting Stanford's introductory humanities program known as Western Culture because it lacked diversity. But that slogan encapsulates one of the main goals of the Progressives.

Public Reason or the Reasonable Consensus would call for the dismantling of the institutions that constitute the foundations of Western civilization, above all the traditional family, the Christian churches, traditional sexual morality, and capitalism. It would dictate that white privilege and systemic racism be overcome by favouring racial minorities. Misogyny and sexism must be overcome by favouring feminism. Homophobia and transphobia must be overcome by promoting LGBTQ causes. Religious superstition should be overcome by recourse to reason. Any historically disadvantaged or oppressed minority must be granted victim status and favoured over any historically privileged class. Any policy or custom that favours Christian principles or values, the traditional family, or traditional sexual morality must be eliminated. Capitalism must be dismantled or transformed and coopted to eliminate inequalities.

It should be clear that the Progressives would decide the ten cases mentioned above against the baker, the doctor, the female athlete, the woman seeking privacy, the parents invoking parental authority, the Chinese student, the Catholic school and Catholic adoption agency, the Christian nurse, and the pro-life speaker. On the other hand, if these cases were decided by judges who based themselves on a traditional understanding of justice according to natural law, they would come to the opposite conclusion in all these cases. In the natural law, it has always been understood that there is a hierarchy of rights and freedoms, and the right to life, the right to religious liberty, the right to the security of one's person, freedom of conscience, and free speech have always stood among the most fundamental. Furthermore, it has always been understood according to natural law that parents are the primary educators of their children and have the right to decide on the education and upbringing they will receive.

---

25   Robert Curry, "'Hey, Hey, Ho, Ho, Western Civ Has Got to Go,'" *Intellectual Takeout*, June 11, 2019, https://www.intellectualtakeout.org/article/hey-hey-ho-ho-western-civ-has-got-go/.

Now it should be stated here that the vast majority of those who hold the Expressive Individualist worldview are not hard core ideologues and do not subscribe to the more radical conclusions that the Progressives arrive at. They rather adhere to the milder version of Expressive Individualism as set out in Chapter 2 and have no wish to see Christianity eliminated or the traditional family destroyed. They have simply absorbed the milder version of Expressive Individualism from the culture and hold to it because it seems logical and convincing and, in many cases, because it is the only worldview they have ever known.

In order for Expressive Individualism to prevail, its adherents must occupy key places in society: judges, legislators, journalists and communications experts, researchers in the social sciences, people with influential positions in government, in left-leaning political parties, and in international bureaucracies, teachers, university professors, community organizers, institutions like Planned Parenthood, NARAL, etc. And indeed, over the years, many Progressives and others ideologically convinced of their agenda have attained positions like these. And of course, they naturally use their positions of authority and power to further their agenda.

For example, Progressive community organizers promote resentment and a desire for liberation among marginalized groups so that they will work towards the subversion of power, patriarchy, and privilege across unjust social institutions. The result has been identity politics: groups claiming victim status setting out grievances and engaging in conflict against dominant groups and against the unjust power structures that support them. They also seek to discredit and cancel historical personages and remove their statues from public places. Another tactic is to ban many of the great works of literature and philosophy of the past, claiming that they are racist, misogynistic, etc. The goal is to discredit and cancel Western civilization as we know it and build a new society, much better than the old.

There has been a move away from classical liberalism, which promoted universal humanism, equality, respect for natural law, and the consideration of people as individuals, to a tendency to see people as members of an oppressed identity group. And these identity groups are not looking merely for tolerance or equality. They seek a transfer of power from corrupt institutions to themselves.

Progressives have also been influential in the dismantling of the traditional family. Up until the early 1960s, both legislation and court decisions were generally based on natural law morality. And this reflected the general social consensus in Western Europe and North America. The use of contraception by married couples was illegal in most states. Abortion was illegal throughout Europe and North America (with some very narrow exceptions in a few countries). There were no gay rights, and adultery as well as the production or distribution of hardcore pornography was considered a crime in all 50 states. Since that time,

Progressives have done everything possible to promote the sexual revolution, which is ultimately aimed at undermining traditional marriage and the family by abolishing sexual taboos in their entirety. Through their efforts, since the end of the Second World War, we have seen the legalization and mainstreaming of contraception, no-fault divorce and abortion, the decriminalization of adultery and hardcore pornography, and the establishment of gay marriage. It has not been a difficult sell. Since people find the fulfillment of their sexual desires to be pleasurable, they will naturally go along with the idea that traditional sexual morality is oppressive and hinders human happiness.

In order to discredit Christianity, there was and continues to be a campaign by progressives to convince people that the Catholic Church's refusal to ordain women to the priesthood is misogynistic, that its ban on contraception is unrealistic and irresponsible, that its refusal to allow divorce is a lack of compassion, that its insistence on a celibate clergy is medieval and cruel, and that its prohibition of sex outside of marriage and homosexual acts should be changed to meet the needs of 21st century men. They label the Catholic Church as being hopelessly out of date and utterly permeated with medieval superstition. And they also maintain that it is a source of division in society and causes wars.

They label Christian moral teaching as subjective religious beliefs and contend that such religious beliefs can't be rationally defended and so are a form of prejudice. They say that insisting on traditional marriage is basically religiously based homophobia, and exempting Catholic adoption agencies from placing children with same-sex couples constitutes a license to engage in unjust discrimination. Such concessions foster bigotry and do damage to society. So traditional moral teaching ends up being branded as hate speech.[26]

The ultimate goal of the more radical and ideologically driven Expressive Individualists is to re-make society by ridding it of religious superstition, outmoded traditional morality, conservative values, and glaring inequalities and to create a prosperous secular utopia of peace, justice, equality, and freedom. They want a new Golden Age, as predicted by Bertrand Russell, a paradise on earth. In the next chapter, we will look at how that is working out and at some of the contradictions inherent in Expressive Individualism.

---

26   Charles Chaput, *Strangers in a Strange Land* (New York, Henry Holt and Company, 2015), 237-238.

Chapter 7

Contradictions

"The further a society drifts from truth, the more it will hate those who speak it."
—attributed to George Orwell (found in a piece by Selwyn Duke)

In Chapter 6, we saw that a major contradiction in Expressive Individualism was its claim to organize society on the basis of the satisfaction of individual preferences without any need for a criterion of justice and morality to settle conflicting preferences and competing rights claims. We noted that, in order to resolve this contradiction, the architects and promoters of Expressive Individualism, those who are most deeply committed to a radically progressive agenda, have opted for a criterion based on the dismantling of traditional morality, the traditional family, and Christianity. They want to create a secular utopia, by which they mean a society based on reason alone and free from religious superstition and traditional, conservative values, a civilization where freedom, justice, peace, happiness, and equality will reign. As we show below, this goal inevitably ends up in further contradictions.

Now, when it comes to secular utopias, humanity's track record has been anything but stellar. And, as we shall see, by their very nature, attempts to create a secular utopia must always end up being totalitarian and intolerant.

The French Revolution was the first attempt in modern times to establish on a grand scale what the revolutionaries hoped would be a secular utopia. Although in its origin the Revolution was not aimed at the Catholic Church as such, in the end it sought to replace Christianity with the cult of the goddess Reason and later with the cult of the Supreme Being, understood as a god who does not interfere in human affairs. As is well known, the French Revolution quickly turned into the Great Terror, where anyone who voiced opposition to the Revolution was to be exterminated. Indeed, modern historians calculate that the revolutionaries killed tens of thousands of people for their opposition to the Revolution.[1]

The 20th century witnessed a number of attempts to establish secular utopias. Adolph Hitler and the Nazi Party in Germany tried to establish one for those of the Aryan or Nordic Master Race. The idea was to overcome divisions in society and create a homogeneous civilization based on racial

---

1   Jennifer Llewellyn and Steve Thompson, "The Reign of Terror," *Alpha History*, July 13, 2023, https://alphahistory.com/frenchrevolution/reign-of-terror/.

purity by uniting all Germans living in historically German territories. Once again, any opposition was crushed, and those who did not form part of the Nordic Master Race were expelled or eliminated, including the murder of 6 million of Europe's Jews.

In Russia in the 20th century, Lenin, followed by Stalin, sought to establish a secular utopia based on Marxism. The Marxist revolution was to be followed by the dictatorship of the proletariat and eventually by a communist society, which would be characterized by common ownership of the means of production and a classless and stateless society with full, universal social equality. Historians calculate that around 60 million people were killed by Lenin and Stalin in their failed attempt to make this dream come true.[2]

In China, Mao Zedong outdid even Lenin and Stalin. Mao saw his revolution as a war on poverty, exploitation, imperialism, and inequality. It was meant to unify the country in line with Mao's version of communism, which saw the peasants in the countryside instead of the urban proletariat as the moving force in the revolution. Historians estimate that at least 80 million Chinese died as a result of Chinese agrarian communism.[3]

In Cambodia between 1975 and 1979, the communist revolution carried out by the Khmer Rouge killed more than 1.7 million people through work, starvation, and torture. Their blueprint for a perfect society: the entire population must adopt the lifestyle of poor agricultural workers. Factories, hospitals, schools, and universities were closed. Qualified professionals were seen as a threat to the regime and either herded into the countryside to work on the land or simply executed.[4]

North Korea is yet another attempt at building a secular paradise which has turned into a nightmare for its inhabitants. Each of its leaders has held that North Korea must remain separate and distinct from the rest of the world, and rely only on its own resources and the guidance of its Dear Leader who has quasi divine status. As a result of this ideology, many have died of starvation and malnutrition and anyone who voices opposition to the regime is executed.[5]

2   R.J. Rummel, "61,911,000 Victims: Utopianism Empowered" in *Lethal Politics: Soviet Genocide and Mass Murder Since 1917* (New Brunswick: Transaction Publishers, 1990), https://www.hawaii.edu/powerkills/USSR.CHAP.1.HTM#:~:text=In%20sum%2C%20probably%20somewhere%20between,of%20this%20number%20is%2061%2C911%2C000.

3   Ilya Somin, "Remembering the biggest mass murder in the history of the world," *The Washington Post*, August 3, 2016, https://www.washingtonpost.com/news/volokh-conspiracy/wp/2016/08/03/giving-historys-greatest-mass-murderer-his-due/.

4   "Cambodia | Holocaust and Genocide Studies," University of Minnesota College of Liberal Arts, April 1, 2019, https://cla.umn.edu/chgs/holocaust-genocide-education/resource-guides/cambodia#:~:text=Lasting%20for%20four%20years%20(between,Rouge%2C%20a%20communist%20political%20group.

5   Eli Fuhrman, "3.5 Million Dead: How North Korea Literally Starved to Death in the 1990s," *The National Interest*, July 25, 2021, https://nationalinterest.org/blog/korea-watch/35-million-dead-how-north-korea-literally-starved-death-1990s-190454.

In each of these cases, power was (and in some cases still is) in the hands of an ideological group committed to the creation of an earthly paradise, and they were (are) prepared to kill as many people as necessary in order to bring about their utopia. The regimes created by those holding these ideologies were not just authoritarian, but rather totalitarian. Regimes are authoritarian when the state simply takes over all political control. It is satisfied with political power and grants its citizens a certain amount of freedom so long as they do not voice opposition to the regime. In a totalitarian regime, on the other hand, the authorities seek to implement an ideology that will bring all aspects of society under their control: the economy, education, art, science, and the personal and moral lives of the citizens. They attempt to control not only the words and actions but even the thoughts of the citizens. A prime example of a fictitious totalitarian state is set out in George Orwell's *1984*.

Those wishing to establish a secular utopia make two fundamental errors. Firstly, as regards those in the Western world, by denying the Christian roots of our civilization and trying to extirpate its Christian elements, they jettison all that constitutes the strength and greatness of our society, leaving it much poorer and weaker. The second error they make is to assume that, given the right worldview and social organization, it is possible to achieve a society that, though not perfect, would be a vast improvement over our present society. Because they lack the Christian doctrine of Original Sin, set out in Chapter 1, they fail to understand man's fallen nature. Hence, the foundation of every attempt to build a utopia is made of sand and is doomed to collapse.

Regimes that try to enforce their blueprint for a secular utopia by their very nature seek to impose their own version of the truth, and everyone is obliged to submit and assent. If the ideal society is to be created, the entire population must be on board, and not a single person or group can be allowed to opt out. So, for a regime like this, dissent is intolerable. Everyone must at least pay lip service to the ideology and not do anything that contradicts it. Failure to assent is seen as an attack on the regime itself, which identifies itself with its ideology. Even a single person disagreeing with the regime represents a threat. He is seen as a reactionary, an enemy, a counter-revolutionary who is seeking to undermine the regime by proposing an alternative and false worldview. He is perceived as someone who is dominated by irrational prejudices and so is perversely unconvinced by the obvious truth of the regime's ideology. He must consequently be motivated by ignorance, bigotry, rage, or resentment. In effect, if his refusal to kowtow to the regime's ideology were allowed to go unpunished, it would risk passing the message that the regime itself is not completely convinced of its position. And the regime fears that the dissenter may inspire others, saying out loud what many others are in fact thinking, thereby calling the whole structure into question.[6]

This is what happened in the Nazi and Communist regimes, where everyone was made to pay lip service to the slogans of the party in power even though very few believed them. A modern-day example is Communist China. Over the years, it has allowed more freedom to its citizens, especially as regards business, the economy, and social life. Yet even today, anyone who voices an opinion that is incompatible with the government's political ideology can easily find himself in prison. For example, around a million practitioners of Falun Gong, a movement that professes a distinct discipline, way of life, and moral philosophy, have been imprisoned in China. Those who do not renounce their beliefs are tortured, and many have been executed. They were not opposing the regime but were simply embracing a different ideology—something that the Communist government could not allow.[7]

The Uyghurs, a Turkish people in Northern China who are mainly Moslem, are also being persecuted. Approximately a million are in concentration camps where they undergo torture if they refuse to abandon certain practices of their Moslem faith. And some Christian groups are also persecuted in China, though not on so great a scale as the Falun Gong and Uyghurs. Essentially, any group that the government does not control and which holds views that might challenge the official party ideology is liable to be persecuted.[8]

Expressive Individualism is going down this same path, and it constitutes one of its glaring contradictions. On the one hand, it purports to be completely neutral and to allow a broad sphere of individual freedom. It advocates a tolerant society where all points of view are welcome. Everyone has the right to hold whatever beliefs or truth claims he desires. Everyone has the right to pursue his own preferences and life project, so long as doing so doesn't interfere with the life project of anyone else. And the government is there to settle conflicting rights claims. On the other hand, as we shall now see, this tolerance of all views and life projects is refused to those who disagree with Expressive Individualism's ideology.

As we saw in Chapter 2, Expressive Individualism claims to be a neutral position that simply allows society to function better. However, as the examination of Expressive Individualism in Chapter 2 made clear, in reality it is a set of dogmas, a substantive belief system about the nature of man, the nature of truth, the nature of morality, and much else. It is essentially a secular

---

6   Thomas Frank, "Liberals want to blame rightwing 'misinformation' for our problems. Get real," *The Guardian*, March 19, 2021, https://www.theguardian.com/commentisfree/2021/mar/19/rightwing-misinformation-liberals.

7   Antonio Graceffo, "Repression of all religions is intensifying in China," *Mercatornet*, May 15, 2023, https://mercatornet.com/repression-of-all-religions-is-intensifying-in-china/84259/.

8   Graceffo, "Repression of all religions is intensifying in China."

religion, a direct alternative to Christianity, which offers a different view on all these subjects and which the ideologues behind Expressive Individualism want to make obligatory for everyone. And, as we also saw in Chapter 2, Expressive Individualism condemns anyone who thinks that he has the truth as being intolerant, dogmatic, narrow-minded, and judgmental. However, Expressive Individualism itself claims to have the truth and will suppress anyone who disagrees.

Those who are most ideologically committed to Expressive Individualism, like all proponents of a secular paradise, hold that it is the most reasonable and rational worldview possible. This is argued to be so because it is based on reason and not on superstition, outmoded customs, or rigid, conservative views of man and society, and hence it is therefore more objective than others. In their view, every reasonable person should consequently agree with it. If the worldview of Expressive Individualism is the only truly rational one, then they view anyone who perversely does not agree with it as irrational, hopelessly mired in religious superstition, white privilege, homophobia, transphobia, misogyny, sexism, heteronormativity, or systemic racism, and probably all of the above. They are the reprobates, the *deplorables*[9] lamented by Hilary Clinton. They are those whom Barrack Obama dismissively referred to as people "who cling to their guns or religion."[10] They cannot be tolerated because their views constitute a threat to the secular paradise that the ideologues behind Expressive Individualism want to establish. The deplorables must be re-educated or suppressed and their views caricatured and trivialized. There can be no live and let live policy. They must be compelled to violate their conscience. Expressive Individualism preaches tolerance and acceptance. But, as it turns out, tolerance is only extended to those who agree with Expressive Individualism. It cannot be extended to dissenters.

Now it should be immediately obvious that Expressive Individualism is gradually moving towards a repressive model. People who do not agree with Expressive Individualism's stance on abortion, same-sex marriage, divorce, euthanasia, transgender rights, the use of pronouns, etc., are intimidated, and if this fails to silence them, they are punished. They are not executed. But they lose their jobs, or are fined, or in some cases, even jailed. Those pushing the agenda of Expressive Individualism have not yet attained complete political control and an independent judiciary at times restrains them. But they use whatever means they can to enforce their worldview. Depending on the

---

9   On Sept. 9, 2016, Hillary Clinton said, "To be grossly generalistic, you can put half of Trump supporters into what I call the 'basket of deplorables' -- right? Racist, sexist, homophobic, xenophobic, Islamophobic, you name it."

10   Ed Pilkington, "Obama angers midwest voters with guns and religion remark," *The Guardian*, April 14, 2008, https://www.theguardian.com/world/2008/apr/14/barackobama.uselections2008.

country in question, they make use of legislators favourable to their cause, or sympathetic judges, the big tech companies, social media, popular culture, the entertainment industry, academia, and public opinion.

In this, Expressive Individualism has departed from classical, natural law liberalism. Classical liberals understood that in a diverse and pluralistic society, accommodation and compromise were necessary and that free speech and minority rights had to be protected. A culture of true tolerance needs to be built if one is going to avoid polarization and foster national unity. This classical liberal understanding of tolerance meant that even though certain ideas or practices were wrong, they should still be tolerated in cases where suppressing them would bring about a greater evil. A typical example often cited was prostitution, where it was thought that completely suppressing the practice would lead to violence against women. As we have just shown, the ideology of Expressive Individualism has no use for this concept. On the one hand, all ideas and practices favoured by Expressive Individualism must not only be tolerated but also wholeheartedly affirmed and celebrated. One must not judge the idea or practice as wrong in any way. And on the other hand, there can be no tolerance for those who disagree with Expressive Individualism.

Shortly before his death in 2015, Roman Catholic Cardinal Francis George of Chicago said, "I expect to die in bed, my successor will die in prison and his successor will die a martyr in the public square."[11] At the time, many scoffers belittled this statement as a gross exaggeration. However, as time goes by, we are seeing just how intolerant Expressive Individualism has become. Here we will give only a few of the many hundreds of examples that could be cited. These illustrate how Expressive Individualism deals with dissenters.

In 2015, Kim Davis, a county clerk in Kentucky, refused to issue marriage licenses to gay couples wanting to get married, saying that she had a religious objection in conscience to gay marriage. For this she was jailed.[12]

In 2020, Leslie Neal-Boylan, the dean of the nursing school at the University of Massachusetts-Lowell, was fired. Her crime? In an email about the violent protests sparked by the BLM movement, she wrote, "Black Lives Matter, but also, everyone's life matters."[13]

---

11   Tim Drake, "Cardinal George: The Myth and Reality of 'I'll Die in My Bed'," *National Catholic Register,* April 17, 2015, https://www.ncregister.com/blog/cardinal-george-the-myth-and-reality-of-ill-die-in-my-bed.

12   Alan Blinder and Tamar Lewin, "Clerk in Kentucky Chooses Jail Over Deal on Same-Sex Marriage," *New York Times,* September 4, 2015, https://www.nytimes.com/2015/09/04/us/kim-davis-same-sex-marriage.html.

13   Madison Dibble, "Dean of Massachusetts nursing school fired after saying 'everyone's life matters.'," *Washington Examiner,* July 2, 2020, https://www.washingtonexaminer.com/news/dean-of-massachusetts-nursing-school-fired-after-saying-everyones-life-matters.

Brendan Eich, the CEO of Mozilla, was forced to resign on April 3, 2014, because it was discovered that in 2008 he had made a $1,000 contribution to support a proposition to ban gay marriage in California.[14]

In 2016, Richard Page was a British magistrate working in a family law court. He was fired for maintaining in an interview that there is insufficient evidence that placing a child in the care of a same-sex couple can be as beneficial to a child as placing them with a husband and wife.[15]

On August 7, 2017, Google engineer James Damore was fired for writing a memo arguing that Google had gone overboard in its efforts to promote diversity. He maintained that women were under represented among the engineers at Google because women are simply less interested in software engineering and not because of discrimination.[16]

Trinity Western University, located in British Columbia, Canada, requires its students to commit themselves to certain Christian ethical standards. As a result of this, in 2018, its application to begin a law school and have its graduates recognized by provincial law societies was refused.[17]

Speakers who are invited to university campuses are regularly shouted down and prevented from delivering their address if it is thought that they might question aspects of Expressive Individualism. When the speakers and their supporters call for free speech to be protected, they are told that there is no right to engage in hate speech and that any calling into question of Expressive Individualism is in fact hate speech.[18]

The Little Sisters of the Poor is a religious congregation of Catholic nuns in the U.S. President Obama's health care law would have forced them to fund contraceptives for their employees—something that goes directly against their religious convictions. After nine years of legal battles, the nuns succeeded in winning an exemption from the contraceptive mandate. However, on the campaign trail, U.S. President Joe Biden said that if elected, he would reinstate

14   Susanna Kim, "Mozilla CEO Brendan Eich Resigns After Protests from Gay Marriage Supporters," *ABC News*, April 11, 2014, https://abcnews.go.com/Business/mozilla-ceo-resigns-calif-gay-marriage-ban-campaign/story?id=23181711.

15   "Magistrate sacked for opposing same-sex adoption is suspended by NHS," The Guardian, March 27, 2016, https://www.theguardian.com/society/2016/mar/27/magistrate-sacked-for-opposing-same-sex-adoption-is-suspended-by-nhs.

16   Timothy Lee, "Google fired James Damore for a controversial gender memo," Ars Technica, January 9, 2018, https://arstechnica.com/tech-policy/2018/01/lawsuit-goes-after-alleged-anti-conservative-bias-at-google/.

17   Kathleen Harris, "Trinity Western loses fight for Christian law school as court rules limits on religious freedom 'reasonable.'," CBC News, June 15, 2018, https://www.cbc.ca/news/politics/trinity-western-supreme-court-decision-1.4707240.

18   Stephen J. Wermiel and Josh Blackman, "Thwarting Speech on College Campuses," American Bar Association, https://www.americanbar.org/groups/crsj/publications/human_rights_magazine_home/the-ongoing-challenge-to-define-free-speech/thwarting-speech-on-college-campuses/.

Obama-era policies requiring the sisters to ensure access to birth control in violation of their religious beliefs.[19]

The Labor Government in the state of Victoria, Australia, has made it a criminal offence, punishable by several years' imprisonment, for a person to pray with another person about issues they are having concerning their sexual orientation or gender identity. It will not be a defence that the person actually wanted prayer.[20]

In 2021, the Liberal Government of Canada enacted Bill C-6, which criminalizes conversion therapy, which includes any "practice, treatment or service designed to change a person's sexual orientation to heterosexual, to change a person's gender identity to cisgender or to repress or reduce non-heterosexual attraction or sexual behaviour or non-cisgender gender expression." So, if a mother encourages her daughter to recognize her body as a beautiful gift from God, or if a preacher preaches a homily on biblical sexual morality with a minor present, the mother or the preacher could be found criminally responsible and be sentenced to five years in prison.[21]

Jack Phillips is a baker and the owner of Masterpiece Cakeshop in Colorado. In 2012, he declined a request to create a wedding cake celebrating a same-sex marriage. He explained that he would be happy to design a cake for the customers for a different event or sell them anything else in his shop. But he does not create cakes expressing messages or celebrating events that conflict with his deeply held religious beliefs. Despite two legal victories, including one at the Supreme Court, the Colorado cake artist now faces a third lawsuit.[22] This follows the logic of those who wish to create a secular utopia. Not a single person can be allowed to opt out, and anyone who tries will be hounded and persecuted until he submits.

Thus, a first contradiction in Expressive Individualism is that in spite of proclaiming tolerance for all points of view, it refuses to extend that tolerance to anyone who disagrees with it.

A second glaring contradiction is the way Expressive Individualism treats the most vulnerable members of society. An earthly paradise would be one where the vulnerable were protected. And the Do No Harm principle and the Golden Rule both dictate that the most vulnerable should receive the full protection of the law. But as we will now see, in the secular utopia envisioned by those who

19   "Joe Biden vs. the Nuns," *Wall Street Journal*, July 9, 2020, https://www.wsj.com/articles/joe-biden-vs-the-nuns-11594336792.

20   Change or Suppression (Conversion) Practices Prohibition Act 2021 (legislation.vic.gov.au).

21   Government Bill (House of Commons) C-4 (44-1) - Royal Assent - An Act to amend the Criminal Code (conversion therapy) - Parliament of Canada

22   Ashley Michels, "Baker back in court after refusing transgender customer," *Fox 31*, October 5, 2022, https://kdvr.com/news/local/baker-back-in-court-after-refusing-transgender-customer/.

espouse Expressive Individualism, the vulnerable are not allowed to benefit from these two principles. We can start with children, who are the most innocent and most defenseless of human beings.

As the Church has taught for over 2,000 years, we can only live a full life and flourish as human beings when we make a gift of ourselves to others, following the natural moral law. Expressive Individualism's emphasis on autonomy is diametrically opposed to this understanding of the human person. It leads people to put their own preferences in first place. As we saw in Chapter 2, some of the natural consequences of this attitude are abortion, divorce, and transgender rights. And all three are devastating as regards children.

Abortion, of course, kills the unborn child in the womb. Advances in the science of genetics have made it clear that the unborn child has a genetic make-up distinct from that of either of its parents from the moment of conception and so possesses all the attributes of a human being from that first moment. So, the pro-abortion lobby has stopped maintaining that the unborn child is not a human being and has instead adopted a definition of personhood that depends on autonomy. So, in Expressive Individualism one only becomes a person, a subject of human rights, once one has attained autonomy. Since the unborn child does not possess autonomy, it has no right to life.[23]

Of course, a recently born child does not have autonomy either, and only acquires it gradually over its first few years of life. Peter Singer, a well-known bioethicist at Princeton, follows this reasoning to its logical conclusion. In his book, *Practical Ethics*, he states: "Human babies are not born self-aware, or capable of grasping that they exist over time. They are not persons." But animals are self-aware, and therefore, "the life of a newborn is of less value than the life of a pig, a dog, or a chimpanzee." In his work entitled *Should the Baby Live?* he advocates that parents should be allowed a period of 28 days after birth to keep or kill their baby. He says that the parents, together with their physicians, have the right to decide "whether the infant's life will be so miserable or so devoid of minimal satisfaction that it would be inhumane or futile to prolong life."[24] This is among the next steps that the abortion lobby is pushing for. It has already scored a victory in those states where children of botched abortions who are born alive can be legally killed by the doctor performing the abortion.[25]

---

23   Nancy Jecker, "What is 'personhood'? The ethics question that needs a closer look in abortion debates," *The Conversation*, May 13, 2022, https://theconversation.com/what-is-personhood-the-ethics-question-that-needs-a-closer-look-in-abortion-debates-182745.

24   Nat Hentoff, "A Professor Who Argues for Infanticide," The Washington Post, September 11, 1999, https://www.washingtonpost.com/archive/opinions/1999/09/11/a-professor-who-argues-for-infanticide/cce7dc81-3775-4ef6-bfea-74cd795fc43f/; Alex Schadenberg, "Philosopher Peter Singer on euthanasia and killing newborns", Euthanasia Prevention Coalition, May 30, 2023, https://alexschadenberg.blogspot.com/2023/05/philosopher-peter-singer-on-euthanasia.html.

25   "Questions and Answers on Born-Alive Abortion Survivors", Charlotte Lozier Institute, January 27, 2023, https://lozierinstitute.org/questions-and-answers-on-born-alive-abortion-survivors/.

Therefore, abortion kills an innocent child. It is true that the expecting mother is also often a victim, and an unplanned pregnancy and unwanted child can constitute a real tragedy in the life of a woman. But this tribulation, great as it might be, can never justify the killing of an innocent person. The Do No Harm principle and the Golden Rule both forbid it. But in Expressive Individualism those principles must be set aside in favour of the absolute autonomy of the mother.

Divorce is also devastating for children. Extensive research published over the past thirty years has shown conclusively that many children are psychologically and emotionally scarred for life by the divorce of their parents, even in the case of low conflict divorces where both parents continue to love and care for them.[26] One study found that 20% of children of divorce required psychiatric care as a child or adolescent, while only one in fifty (2%) in the comparison group had received such care. Other studies have shown that children of divorced parents are far more likely to engage in substance abuse, to suffer from depression, to drop out of school, to be abused by a parent's new partner or to commit crimes and be jailed. There is a vast amount of social science research showing that children do best when they are raised in a stable home with their biological parents.[27]

Once again, in light of these findings, the Do No Harm principle and the Golden Rule both dictate that the parents should make every effort to form a stable family life together in order to avoid doing serious damage to their children. But in Expressive Individualism the autonomy of the parents takes precedence over the well-being of the children, and so no-fault divorce, or divorce on demand, has become the norm in most states.

A third area where Expressive Individualism harms children is in its embrace of transgender ideology, which holds that each person has a 'gender identity' (an internal sense of gender), which may or may not align with their biological sex. Transgender people identify as something other than their biological sex. They may struggle to accept their male or female bodies and choose to undergo

---

26   Leila Miller, *Primal Loss: The Now-Adult Children of Divorce Speak* (n.p.: LCB Publishing, 2017); Andrew Root, *The Children of Divorce (Youth, Family, and Culture): The Loss of Family as the Loss of Being* (Ada: Baker Academic, 2010); Bryce J. Christensen and Nicole M. King, "New Research," *The Family in America 27*, no. 1 (2013); Teresia Ångarne-Lindberg and Marie Wadsby, "Psychiatric and Somatic Health in Relation to Experience of Parental Divorce in Childhood," *International Journal of Social Psychiatry* 58, no. 1 (2012), 16-25; Patrick F. Fagan and Aaron Churchill, "The Effects of Divorce on Children," Marriage & Religion Research Institute, January 11, 2012, https://marri.us/wp-content/uploads/The-Effects-of-Divorce-on-Children.pdf.

27   Anna Sarkadi, Robert Kristiansson, Frank Oberklaid, and Sven Bremberg, "Fathers' Involvement and Children's Developmental Outcomes: A Systematic Review of Longitudinal Studies," *Acta Paediatrica* 97, no. 2 (2008), 153-8; Athena Yenko, "Divorce-alternate week arrangement damages children, experts say," *International Business Times*, June 26, 2014, https://www.ibtimes.com.au/divorce-alternate-week-arrangement-damages-children-expert-says-1345130.

medical treatment to alter their sex. They will often say that they are 'trapped in the wrong body.'

Studies have shown that up to 94 percent of children who experience gender confusion or gender dysphoria will become comfortable with their own bodies after passing through puberty without interventions.[28] It should be obvious enough that the best way to help these children is psychological counselling or simply leaving them to work out their gender confusion on their own. However, Expressive Individualism's insistence on absolute autonomy, even for children, takes exactly the opposite approach. It recommends the administration of puberty blockers to these children and even sex-change operations, the consequences of which the children will have to live with for their whole lives. Children have been started on puberty-blockers as young as nine, and under the 'guidance' of gender 'experts' girls have been allowed to consent to double mastectomies as young as age 13.[29]

More and more laws are making it illegal for parents to oppose the gender choice of their children, threatening them with the loss of custody and even jail.[30] Medical personnel are instructed to report parents who refuse to affirm their child's new gender to Child Protection Services and schools are directed to investigate parents who oppose a child's transition. In some school districts, children are taught that gender is fluid and are encouraged to ask themselves whether they feel that their gender matches with their biological sex. In this way the school system preys on those children who are insecure, fragile and given to self-doubt.

Another tactic is to tell parents that the child is at an increased risk for suicide unless they affirm the child's gender choice, thereby pressuring parents to go against their deeply held instinct to protect their children. They are cajoled into leaving them in the hands of therapists and doctors who will drug and sterilize them and surgically correct their sex, confident that they know best what is good for other people's children.

Studies have also shown that gender dysphoria among children is often the result of psychological and emotional trauma. For example, a 2018 U.S. study found that prior to the onset of their gender dysphoria, over 60% of minors had been diagnosed with at least one mental health disorder or neurodevelopmental disability.

---

28   "Gender Dysphoria in Children," American College of Pediatricians, November, 2018, https://acpeds.org/position-statements/gender-dysphoria-in-children.

29   Mercatornet: *Chloe's story: puberty blockers at 13, a double mastectomy at 15.* https://mercatornet.com/chloe-cole-gender-transition/80073/. NIH National Library of Medicine: *Gender affirming medical care of transgender youth.* https://www.ncbi.nlm.nih.gov/pmc/articles/PMC8496167/.

30   Virginia Allen, "New Canadian Law Could Send Parents to Jail for Not Affirming Gender Identity," *The Daily Signal,* February 11, 2022, https://www.dailysignal.com/2022/02/11/new-canadian-law-could-send-parents-to-jail-for-not-affirming-gender-identity/.

Again, when faced with a child who suffers from a mental health disorder and who is asking for gender transition, the logical response should be to have the child undergo therapy to deal with the mental health disorder. However, increasingly such children are ushered into a regime of puberty blockers and sex change operations. All this can only be described as horrific child abuse. As Tyler O'Neil has shown in his article, "Detransitioners Open Up About How Transgender 'Medicine' Left Them Scarred for Life"[31] more and more of those who have de-transitioned are telling their tragic stories, and it is truly heartbreaking. And yet, those pushing for the earthly paradise envisioned by Expressive Individualism are determined to continue and even expand the number of children who undergo gender transition. In essence, children are considered expendable. They can be sacrificed at the altar of the ideology of Expressive Individualism.

Apart from children, other people who are particularly vulnerable are the elderly, infirm, and others suffering from various physical and mental disabilities. According to the logic of Expressive Individualism, which embraces the Golden Rule and the Do No Harm principle, these people should receive the full protection of the law. However, the Euthanasia movement, which originally justified itself on the principle of autonomy, has turned against these vulnerable people and seeks to eliminate them. Originally, euthanasia was legalized exclusively for people who were suffering from a terminal illness and who wanted to avoid the months of suffering they would inevitably have to undergo before eventually dying. By virtue of the principle of autonomy, it was held that these people could make an informed choice and consent to be euthanized. However, even when someone who has his full mental capacity decides to end his life through euthanasia, it can often constitute a selfish act. It can have a devastating effect on his family and on his social circle, who may well feel guilty in that they have failed to provide him with the support that he required.

As we saw in Chapter 1, in the Christian worldview, all euthanasia is totally unacceptable, even when someone has full mental capacity to decide. Christianity teaches that human life is sacred since it involves the creative action of God, and the human person has a special relationship with God, who is its sole end. The Creator is the Lord of life and death, and no one may arrogate to himself the right to directly destroy an innocent human being nor take his own life. In any event, modern medicine has developed techniques

---

31 Tyler O'Neil, "Detransitioners Open up About How Transgender 'Medicine' Left Them Scarred for Life," *PJ Media*, March 12, 2021, "https://pjmedia.com/news-and-politics/tyler-o-neil/2021/03/12/detransitioners-open-up-transgender-identity-was-a-way-to-cope-with-my-trauma-and-body-hatred-n1432065.

of palliative care so that no one is obliged to suffer unbearable pain during a terminal illness. But in fact, many of those who ask for euthanasia suffer from depression or some other form of mental illness and are in no position to make an informed decision on this question. Many are pressured by their families, insurers, and medical personnel to end their lives so as not to be a burden, financial or otherwise, on their families or the health system. For example, insurance companies sometimes tell their clients that they won't pay for extended medical care but will pay the full cost of the euthanasia procedure. And palliative care clinics that refuse to euthanize their patients risk being defunded or decertified.[32]

It is also becoming more frequent that disabled or terminally ill people who are judged by law incapable of making the decision to undergo euthanasia, even young children, are put to death with the consent of their family. In 2021 the Canadian Parliament enacted legislation that would allow people whose only underlying medical condition is a mental illness to receive MAID (Medical Assistance in Dying). This was to come into effect in March 2023, but just before it did, the Liberal government paused it due to widespread concerns over possible consequences. No new date for its implementation has been set.[33]

So once again we have a situation where the Golden Rule and the Do No Harm principle are being set aside and innocent people whom the law should protect are killed to satisfy the preferences of those with full autonomy and the power to enforce their will.

The move of Expressive Individualism towards intolerance can be seen in its attempts to control thought and expression. Autonomy and equality mean that each one's life project and worldview must be respected. However, as we saw above, any opinion, expression or worldview not in conformity with Expressive Individualism is considered illegitimate, a form of harassment, an egregious violation of equal respect and so cannot itself benefit from the protection afforded by the principle of equal respect. So the diversity and tolerance that Expressive Individualism preaches exclude anyone with traditional opinions on morality and, as we are witnessing, calls for speech codes and obligatory sensitivity training in proper opinions and attitudes. In Canada, if one makes a negative remark about any of the basic principles of Expressive Individualism that someone else finds offensive, even in a private conversation, he can be dragged before a human rights tribunal to answer charges of discrimination, inciting hatred, etc. And it becomes almost impossible to refute an allegation of micro-aggression, since the only criterion

---

32   The Delta Hospice Society lost its funding from the British Columbia Provincial Government because it refused to allow its patients to be euthanized on its premises.

33   Eligibility for medical assistance in dying for persons suffering solely from mental illness extended to March 17, 2024 - Canada.ca

for guilt is subjective: whether the complainant felt offended by whatever it is that you said.

A final contradiction inherent in Expressive Individualism that we can mention is the fact that, even though the secular utopia that it seeks to create is supposed to result in an earthly paradise of freedom, justice, peace, happiness, and equality, in fact for many it has delivered shattered lives, broken, and disillusioned people wracked by loneliness and the bitterness that inevitably results from worldly indulgence.[34] Expressive Individualism tells people that the happiness offered by the world is the only happiness that is worth pursuing. It rules out any appeal to transcendence.

This gives rise to a deeper problem that Cardinal Newman identified as incurable loneliness.

> More than separating someone from his or her hometown… the world's unfulfilled and unfulfillable promises of happiness end up separating a person not only from God but also from the world itself. The world is self-alienating. For a season, buying into the world's promises of happiness seems the best use of time, money, effort and love. But eventually the repetition of pleasures and amusements emerges for what it always was: a surface distraction against inner loneliness, aggravated by the very diversions themselves.[35]

In his classic poem, *Dover Beach*, the poet Matthew Arnold expressed the empty allure of the world as follows:

> …for the world, which seems
> To lie before us like a land of dreams
> So various, so beautiful, so new,
> Hath neither joy, nor love, nor light,
> Nor certitude, nor peace, nor help for pain …[36]

At the heart of this contradiction is the fact that Expressive Individualism's understanding of the human person is deeply flawed. We have already mentioned the fact that it ignores the crucial factor of man's fallen human nature and believes in unlimited human progress.

---

34   Thomas Likona, "The Neglected Heart: The Emotional Dangers of Premature Sexual Involvement," *CERC Catholic Education Resource Centre*, n.d., https://www.catholiceducation.org/en/marriage-and-family/sexuality/the-neglected-heart-the-emotional-dangers-of-premature-sexual-involvement.html.

35   John Henry Hanson, *Home Again: A Prayerful Rediscovery of Your Catholic Faith* (New York: Scepter Publishers, 2020), 139-140.

36   Matthew Arnold, "Dover Beach", in *Poetical Works of Matthew Arnold* (London: Macmillan & Co., 1892), 226-227.

We also saw in Chapter 4 that man does have a human nature and there is a natural moral law, in spite of Expressive Individualism's denial of same. And in accordance with our human nature, we can only lead a full life in the measure that we give of ourselves to others, leading a life of service. Expressive Individualism's emphasis on autonomy leads to self-centeredness, which is the opposite of self-giving and which can only result in loneliness, sadness, depression, etc. Expressive Individualism declares that we are absolutely free. But freedom makes no sense and cannot fulfill one unless one has meaning in one's life. One needs an ideal to pursue in order to have something to use one's freedom for.

It is true, of course, that those who espouse Expressive Individualism can use their autonomy to make wise choices. Many lead noble and virtuous lives. They are faithful to their spouse and children, assume their professional and civic responsibilities, engage in charitable work, etc. However, the message of Expressive Individualism leads many people astray. When they are told that they are free to exercise their autonomy in whichever way they wish, many will tend to lead selfish lives.

This point is well illustrated in the 1993 movie *Groundhog Day*, one of the truly great films to come out of Hollywood. In the movie, Bill Murray plays Phil Connors, a Pittsburgh weatherman who thinks he is the greatest and most talented person around. He is an arrogant cynic, contemptuous of almost everyone else. He goes with his cameraman and also with his producer Rita (to whom he is sexually attracted) to cover the groundhog story and groundhog festival in Punxsutawney, PA, at which a real groundhog comes out of his hole on February 2 to reveal how much longer winter will last. Rita tells him that people love the groundhog story. He answers that people are morons. She tells him "You are missing all the fun. People have been partying all night'". He answers, "they are hicks, Rita." He records his report when the groundhog emerges and then heads home. But is stopped by a snow storm and has to go back to stay overnight in a bed and breakfast run by people he would consider nice hicks.

On the next morning, it is February 2 all over again. He spends 10 years in a time warp reliving the same day. When he realizes that he is not crazy and that he can live forever and do anything without consequences (not get sick, not go to jail, not get fat, not die, not get punished), he indulges all his whims, caprices, and passions: pastries, cigarettes, sex with young local women, etc. He also tries everything he can to have sex with Rita. But all in vain. She won't have him because she realizes that, in spite of all his subterfuges, at heart, he is a shallow and selfish person. Indeed, indulging his passions doesn't make him happy. On the contrary, he falls into deep depression and tries multiple times to commit suicide. This is the fate of those who buy into the promise of hedonism held out by Expressive Individualism. But he can't even kill himself.

He still wakes up every morning on the same day. He gradually realizes that he is an obnoxious person and that Rita is a good person—far, far better than he is. With this, he also slowly realizes that what makes life worth living is not what you get from it but what you put into it. So he begins to help the locals. He reads poetry and learns piano, no longer to impress Rita but for its own sake. He catches a boy who falls out of a tree every day. He gets coffee for Rita and Larry, the cameraman, and takes a genuine interest in Larry whom he had originally considered a moron. He begins to be nice to a guy he meets on the stairs each morning.

By the end of the film, he is no longer obsessed with getting Rita into bed. He realizes that she is a truly wonderful and virtuous person and has fallen in love with her without reservation and without hope that she will ever love him in return. Only in the end, when he has completely given up hope, does he finally win the woman he loves. Not by having sex with her, but by getting her to love him and marry him. And she finally does fall in love with him because he is now a changed man. Much improved. And with her love, it is finally February 3. He escapes the curse when he blesses the day he has just lived, having filled it with self-giving and service. He escapes it when he is truly able to say with sincerity that this day has been the most wonderful and fulfilling day of his life. His transformation and redemption contradict everything that Expressive Individualism tells us. He is not liberated by becoming more authentic or by acting on whims and urges. He does the opposite. He learns to appreciate the country hicks and the community. He resolves to become a better person by giving himself totally to others: learning to sculpt ice and play music to entertain others, spending the day doing large and small favours for others, and getting rid of his arrogance and cynicism.

The human person also has a natural yearning for the transcendent. We are hardwired to believe in a higher power. As Augustine put it, addressing God, "You have made us for yourself, Lord, and our hearts are restless until they rest in You."[37] In the long history of humanity, there has never existed an atheistic culture. The denial of transcendence by Expressive Individualism has negatively affected our society, preventing many people from leading a full life, a life that leads to true happiness.

Expressive Individualism promises a Brave New World of hedonism: free sex, unlimited access to entertainment, the latest technologies, and consumer goods; economic prosperity; freedom to do and be whatever one wishes; etc. But these things can never fulfill the deepest yearnings of the human heart. They leave one empty. In Western Europe and North America, the result is an

---

37   Augustine of Hippo, *The Confessions* (New York: Doubleday, 1960) Book 1, p. 1.

epidemic of loneliness,[38] substance abuse,[39] suicide,[40] depression,[41] and other pathologies among those who do not profess any religion.

Inevitably, Expressive Individualism is glaringly inconsistent and is beset by major contradictions. It cannot deliver the secular utopia it promises. The Christian worldview, on the other hand, is entirely consistent. It presents a perfectly coherent explanation of man and the world. And, contrary to Expressive Individualism it leads to human flourishing and happiness. In our final chapter, we will examine how someone holding the Christian worldview can best navigate a world dominated by Expressive Individualism.

38   Barbara Kay, "Loneliness is a human catastrophe – and it's getting worse," *National Post,* August 7, 2019, https://nationalpost.com/opinion/barbara-kay-loneliness-is-a-human-catastrophe-and-its-getting-worse; Jean Twenge, "Less in-person social interaction with peers among U.S. adolescents in the 21st century and links to loneliness," *Journal of Social and Personal Relationships,* 36, no. 6; "Loneliness among Older Adults: A National Survey of Adults 45+," *AARP The Magazine,* September, 2010, https://assets.aarp.org/rgcenter/general/loneliness_2010.pdf.

39   Andrew Kolodny et al., "The Prescription Opioid and Heroin Crisis: A Public Health Approach to an Epidemic of Addiction," *Annual Review of Public Health* 36, (2015), 559-574.

40   Jamie Ducharme, "U.S. Suicide Rates Are the Highest They've Been Since World War II," *Time Magazine,* June 20, 2019, https://time.com/5609124/us-suicide-rate-increase/.

41   A. H. Weinberger et al., "Trends in depression prevalence in the USA from 2005 to 2015: widening disparities in vulnerable groups," *Psychological Medicine* 48, no. 8 (2017), 1308-1315, https://pubmed.ncbi.nlm.nih.gov/29021005/; Maggie Fox, "Major depression on the rise among everyone, new data shows," *NBC News,* May 10, 2018, https://www.nbcnews.com/health/health-news/major-depression-rise-among-everyone-new-data-shows-n873146.

Chapter 8

Where Do We Go From Here?

"The times are never so bad that a good man can't live in them."
—St. Thomas More

"How small of all that human hearts endure, that part which
laws or kings can cause or cure!"
—Samuel Johnson

The question we must now address is: How is a Christian going to live in a society in which Expressive Individualism reigns supreme? If he articulates his own values, he risks losing his job, being fined, and, if he persists in spite of judicial warnings, he may well find himself in jail for contempt of court.

One alternative is to keep his head down, avoid speaking about controversial subjects, and just toe the line if he is pressured to do so. This can come about, for example, if all employees are asked to wear a rainbow pin during Gay Pride month or are asked to donate to an LGBTQ cause, or if they are asked in public for an opinion on one of the hot button issues. He might think, "Well after all, what is the harm of expressing an opinion I disagree with in order to avoid complicating my life and risk losing my job?" What is the harm? What is the harm with parroting preposterous slogans if, by doing so, I will stay out of trouble? That is indeed the question.

In the year 250 AD, the Roman Emperor Decius issued a decree requiring everyone in the Roman Empire to publicly offer sacrifice or burn incense to the Roman gods. It was intended as a sign of loyalty to the Emperor and the Empire. Those who complied were given a certificate. Those who refused would be imprisoned, tortured, and executed. Now, in conscience, a Christian could not offer sacrifice or burn incense to false gods. Many Christians simply went into hiding or fled to places where the decree was not being systematically enforced. But those who were unlucky enough to be required to offer sacrifice and who refused were indeed executed. Some Christians did comply with the decree. These so-called Certificate Christians maintained that they should remain in good standing with the Church in spite of having offered incense. They contended that, even though they had offered incense to the Roman gods in public, in their hearts they remained Christians and did not believe in the Roman gods. This stance was rejected by the Church, and these Certificate Christians who had offered incense were considered apostates and expelled from the Church, although if they repented, they were later accepted back after having performed a penance that was imposed on them.[1]

Why was the Church so severe with these Certificate Christians? It was essentially because the Church understood that the Christian cannot lead a double life and is called to give a public witness to his faith. As Christ said,

> You are the salt of the earth... you are the light of the world, A city set on a hill cannot be hid. Nor do men light a lamp and put it under a bushel, but on a stand, and it gives light to all in the house. Let your light so shine before men, that they may see your good works and give glory to your Father who is in heaven.[2]

Thus, we are called to bear witness to our faith, since it is through the witness of our lives that others will come to believe and find salvation as well. If the Apostles had hunkered down in Jerusalem after Our Lord's Ascension instead of going out to preach the Gospel, Christianity would have quickly disappeared. So, they launched out to preach, and all but one were martyred for the Faith.

Rod Dreher's book *Live Not By Lies* argues that Václav Havel's most famous injunction to would-be dissidents was to "live in truth." Havel wrote about the power of the powerless, referring to the case of a grocer who is told to post a sign in his shop bearing the slogan from the Communist Manifesto, "Workers of the world, unite!" This act confirms that this is what is expected of one in a communist society and perpetuates the belief that this is what it means to be a good citizen. When he removes the sign, the grocer breaks the rules of the game by refusing to mouth a lie, thereby showing that it is possible to live within the truth in spite of persecution.

Havel argues that living in truth and not by lies is necessary to maintain one's self-respect and sense of responsibility. He quotes those of the Soviet bloc who suffered for the faith, saying that there was no other way out. Christians know that it is better to die for their faith than to betray Christ. Havel states that a person who lives only for his own comfort and survival and who is willing to live within a lie to protect that is a demoralized person. The system depends on this demoralization, deepens it, "and is in fact a projection of it into society," he writes. "Living within the truth, as humanity's revolt against an enforced position, is, on the contrary, an attempt to regain control over one's own sense of responsibility."[3]

The question we posed above was: What is the harm with paying lip service to preposterous slogans if, by doing so, I will stay out of trouble? But there

---

1   Paul Kroll, "Church History: Persecution, Penance and the Lapsed," *Grace Communion International*, n.d., https://www.gci.org/articles/persecution-penance-and-the-lapsed/.

2   Mt. 5:13-16 (Revised Standard Version: Second Catholic Edition),

3   Vaclav Havel, *The Power of the Powerless* (Armonk: M. E. Sharpe; 1985), Ch. IX.

are other questions that go along with that one. Who am I? What do I believe in? What do I stand for? What principles do I hold to? What is the ultimate meaning of my life? It is by answering those questions that we will understand what the harm is with going with the flow and capitulating to Expressive Individualism. As we saw in Chapter 1, the Christian is someone who knows that he is made in the image and likeness of God, redeemed by the Precious Blood of Christ, made a son of God by baptism, called by God in this life to seek personal holiness in Christ through the Church and to be an apostle to others, and ultimately called to eternal happiness with God in heaven. That is the Christian identity. It is who we are. To submit to Expressive Individualism is to live a lie. It is to deny our Christian identity, to betray the deepest truth about who we are. One day, immediately after our death, we will stand before the Supreme Judge and render an account of our life of the choices we made. And, at that point, the question of whether we were true to our Christian identity will loom large.

As lay Christians living in the heart of civil society, we are called to act as salt, light, and leaven, to restore all things in Christ from within the very heart of civil society. This certainly means spreading the Gospel message among our family and friends, insisting on religious freedom, and standing up for our faith when the situation calls for it. But it also means trying to influence the culture so that its values and its laws reflect the natural law.

Christians do not want a theocracy. They do not want the Church to dictate policy to politicians. They do not want Church law or doctrine to be enforced by the state. They do not want to impose their religion on anyone. As we saw in Chapter 5, the separation of Church and State is an idea that was first articulated by the Church itself, and it is one that the Church completely endorses. Furthermore, in its Declaration on Religious Freedom, the Catholic Church has stated that,

> the human person has a right to religious freedom. This freedom means that all men are to be immune from coercion... such that no one is to be forced to act in a manner contrary to his own beliefs, whether privately or publicly, whether alone or in association with others...[4]

However, as we saw in Chapter 4, the laws of the state should reflect the natural law. Issues such as abortion, same-sex marriage, and euthanasia are not religious issues. They pertain to our human nature, to what it means to be a human being.

---

4   Second Vatican Council, "Declaration on Religious Freedom, Dignitatis Humanae," December 7, 1965, sec. 2 (hereafter cited as DH), http://www.vatican.va/archive/hist_councils/ii_vatican_council/documents/vat-ii_decl_19651207_dignitatis-humanae_en.html.

The Christian has a mission: to live a unity of life by making his faith the guiding principle behind all he does, to be an apostle to those of his milieu, and to try to have a positive influence on the culture. This means, for example, working so that the laws respect the sanctity of human life, so that they safeguard the family and protect the vulnerable. It means working to create an environment conducive to raising a family, which does not only mean an environment clean of pornography but a society that is not imbued with hedonism and a contraceptive mentality.

At the same time, it is crucial for the Christian to remember that evil does not lurk "out there" among the Expressive Individualists or others. As Alexander Solzhenitsyn said, "the line separating good and evil runs not through states, nor between classes, nor even between political parties, but right through the center of each human heart."[5] We are all fallen creatures prone to sin. We each have within us a deep well of iniquity. As Chesterton said, "we are all in the same boat, and we are all seasick."[6] We can't change the world without changing ourselves. Personal conversion is a prerequisite for any mission that seeks to make the world a better place. Indeed, we need to be convinced that the real obstacles to the evangelization of our culture are not external: the movements, groups, ideologies, and persons that are opposed to Christianity. The real obstacles are rather internal: our own laziness, our love of comfort, our pride, and human respects, etc.

Pope John Paul II set out the characteristics that Christians should possess:

> There is a need for heralds of the Gospel who are experts in humanity, who have a profound knowledge of the heart of present-day man, participating in his joys and hopes, anguish and sadness, and who are at the same time contemplatives in love with God. For this we need new saints... We must supplicate the Lord to increase the Church's spirit of holiness and send us new saints to evangelize today's world.[7]

As Patrick Madrid has said:

> You are the sower. You sow the seed and God follows behind with his grace to give the increase. He makes you his partner... But God is the one who converts hearts, not you or I. His grace can reach souls in ways we can't understand.

---

5   Aleksandr Solzhenitsyn, *The Gulag Archipelago 1918–1956*, trans. Thomas Whitney (New York: Harper & Row, 1974), Part IV, Chapter 1.

6   Gilbert Chesterton, *What's Wrong With the World* (n.p.: n.p., 1910), Part II, Chapter 2, https://www.gutenberg.org/files/1717/1717-h/1717-h.htm.

7   John Paul II, *Address to the Symposium of European Bishops*, 11 October, 1985, sec. 13, https://www.vatican.va/content/john-paul-ii/en/speeches/1985/october/documents/hf_jp-ii_spe_19851003_radiodiffusione.html.

> It is God who has to do the heavy lifting when it comes to changing
> a person's heart. Only he is able to illuminate hearts and minds with the
> light of his grace. If the conversion of souls were our job and not his, few
> people would ever come to Christ into his church.[8]

Spiritual transformation is the work of the grace. We do not convert souls. The Holy Spirit does. Once a recently ordained priest visited the legendary Archbishop Fulton J. Sheen, who was famed for, among other things, winning many converts to the Catholic Church. Sheen was in the hospital on his deathbed. "Archbishop Sheen," the priest said, "I have come for your counsel. I want to be a convert-making priest like you. I've already won fifteen people to the faith. What is your advice?" Sheen painfully pushed himself up on his elbows from his reclining position and looked the priest in the eye. "The first thing to do," he said, "is to stop counting."[9]

If he is going to draw others to the Faith, the Christian must be immersed in God. He must have a strong union with Christ, a deep spiritual life, and be totally committed to personal holiness, which entails a life of prayer and sacrifice. And, since spiritual progress ultimately depends on the grace of the Holy Spirit rather than our own efforts, daily prayer and sacrifice for those whom he hopes to help spiritually are essential. The Christian's daily life must reflect the attractiveness of the Gospel message. His friends and colleagues should see through his daily example that the Christian faith is a joy to embrace. Indeed, the main reason why people reject Christianity is the abject failure of many Christians to lead morally upright lives. Christian life must always consist in an ongoing and lifelong struggle to overcome our pride, laziness, sensuality, etc. A smug, self-satisfied Christian simply hasn't understood.

The mission also calls for sacrifice. On the one hand, sacrifice means getting out of our comfort zone, overcoming our laziness and self-centeredness, and being with people. Christ is our model. In the Gospels, we see that Our Lord was constantly going about doing good with a great thirst for souls, even when, we might say, he found himself in difficult circumstances that would have justified an inward-looking attitude. As he carries his cross to Calvary, his only words are to console the women weeping over his fate. Once on the Cross, he converts the Good Thief. He didn't isolate himself. In the Gospels, we see him continuously with the crowd, trying to win souls. If I am attached to a soft life of Netflix, golf, following sports, and shopping, I will never be an apostle.

---

8   Patrick Matrid, *Search and Rescue* (Nashua: Sophia Institute Press, 2001), 214.
9   Richard John Neuhaus, *On Rereading the Civil War*, December, 2007, https://www.firstthings.com/article/2007/12/on-rereading-the-civil-war.
10   Jn. 15:20 (Revised Standard Version: Second Catholic Edition).

On the other hand, sacrifice also means that we will have to face opposition. Christ warned the Apostles of this: "A servant is not greater than his master. If they persecuted me, they will persecute you also."[10] And St. Paul reminds his disciple Timothy of this same teaching: "all who want to lead a godly life will be persecuted."[11] As Blessed Alvaro del Portillo, the first successor of Saint Josemaria as head of Opus Dei said:

> He who truly strives to be a good Christian will inevitably meet with difficulties and clash with the paganized environment that is so prevalent today. The same thing happened to Our Lord, and the disciple is not greater than his master. We are in the world but we are notworldly. We are in the world, we live in the world, in order to sanctify it and guide it back to God. Thus we can never adopt the false naturalness of someone who hides his Christianity when the circumstances around him are not favourable; nor can we camouflage ourselves by adopting habits or customs contrary to our Christian vocation. We shun any kind of fanaticism (which can never arise when charity abounds) but neither do we feel inhibited by the clamour of those who behave as enemies of the Cross of Christ, which many still regard as foolishness or a scandal. Don't be afraid of clashing with the paganized morality that so often surrounds you. Show clearly that you are Christian, by your lives, your spirit of service, your hard work, your understanding, your zeal for souls, your cheerfulness.[12]

Although we don't seek out suffering, everyone experiences it. And when we do, it will either break us or make us more holy. We have the choice. Everyone, without exception, receives a cross to bear, but Christians are the only ones who know what to do with it. St. Paul tells us that "for those who love God, all things work together unto the good."[13] We can choose to see necessary suffering as something negative, or we can see it as an opportunity to express our love for God by embracing the cross with love and being grateful because our Father God is treating us as he treated his Son, Jesus Christ. When St Peter and St John were flogged by the Sanhedrin, they rejoiced "that they were counted worthy to suffer dishonor for the name [of Christ]."[14] In *Live Not By Lies*, Rod Dreher quotes many Soviet dissidents who were grateful for having spent years in prison. They found it a liberating experience compared to the ideological prison that Communism imposed on society.

Unlike the dissidents in the Soviet Union or China, we are unlikely to be executed. Yet, as we saw in Chapter 7, there are penalties for speaking the truth.

11   2 Tim. 3:12 (Revised Standard Version: Second Catholic Edition).
12   Alvaro del Portillo, *Unpublished Letter* n.p., February 1, 1991.
13   Rm. 8:28 (Douay-Rheims-Challoner).
14   Acts. 5:40-41 (Revised Standard Version: Second Catholic Edition).

One can lose one's job, be fined, be forced to undergo sensitivity training, and be cancelled on social media. The state may even remove children from the care of their parents. And persistence in saying the truth can, in some cases, land one in jail. And the situation may deteriorate even further.

In light of this, one might be tempted to give up. It seems that the culture war has been lost. The woke architects of Expressive Individualism and their social justice warriors hold power and are hostile to Christianity. It is true that the majority of people are not involved in the social justice crusade. But they don't seem interested in Christianity, God, or the Faith. They seem to live a practical atheism, leading their daily lives as though God does not exist and not giving any thought or consideration to the possibility of an afterlife. And many who call themselves Christians lead immoral lives and give a bad example. It is quite easy to become demoralized, to despair, and to lose all hope. This, however, would be a mistake. Although we should be relentless in carrying out our mission, we do not place our hope in politics or in people. The Christian's ultimate hope should be in Jesus Christ, who overcame death and offers us the glory of heaven. So, the Christian always has hope. No matter how bad the situation may seem, God invites us to a glory that has no end. Remember, to the Apostles, the disciples, and the Holy Women, on Good Friday all seemed lost. But in reality, it was the greatest victory of all time.

There are good reasons to hope that our efforts to spread the faith will bear fruit. On the one hand, as we have mentioned, the earthly paradise promised by Expressive Individualism has turned into a nightmare for many. Hedonism in the form of easy sex, consumer goods, popular entertainment, and the freedom to do and be whatever one wishes can never fulfill the deepest aspirations of the human heart. They result in an empty life and, as we saw in Chapter 7, in an epidemic of loneliness, substance abuse, suicide, depression, and other pathologies among the irreligious.

One basis for our hope is that we know the truth about man, about how to lead a fulfilling and meaningful life and how to truly flourish as a human being. This message is ultimately the most appealing one on offer because it is true. It is the perennial message of the Gospel that "beauty ever ancient, ever new," as Augustine put it.[15]

Another reason for hope is that, as we said above, although there are many social justice warriors, they are far from the majority. Most irreligious people are not hard-core ideologues. They espouse the moderate version of Expressive Individualism that we described in Chapter 2, having absorbed it from the culture. They believe in personal autonomy in the sense that they have a right to decide their own values and embark on a life project. They hold to moral relativism and tolerance towards other views, believing that this is the only way a

---

15   Augustine of Hippo, *The Confessions* (New York: Doubleday, 1960), 220.

society can function without conflict. They agree with the Do No Harm Principle and the Golden Rule. They believe in human rights and equality. They accept that science and reason have made scientific and technological breakthroughs, increased life expectancy, improved health, and raised the standard of living, and so science and reason provide a better guide to living than religion, which is largely superstition.

Many of these irreligious people have absorbed the Expressive Individualist worldview unthinkingly. It is the only worldview they know. The other worldviews that they have heard about, such as Christianity, have been painted very negatively, and so they are not motivated to investigate them. In particular, they know almost nothing about the Christian worldview. Although it is often difficult to engage them on these subjects, once we do, they can be surprisingly open to Christianity. They will have no serious answer to the critique of Expressive Individualism set out in Chapters 4-7. And they often respond positively to the Christian message. In essence, like everyone, they are looking for happiness. And it is not difficult to show that Expressive Individualism leads to an empty life rather than happiness. In fact, even the social justice warriors themselves have no answer to the critique of Expressive Individualism, which is why they are taught to shout down Christians by accusing them of uttering hate speech rather than trying to debate them in rational argument.

A further reason for our hope is that the Holy Spirit is acting in the Church, Christ has assured us that he will be with His Church until the end of time, and has promised that the Gates of Hell will not prevail against it. Throughout her long history the Catholic Church has frequently been faced with powerful enemies bent on destroying Her. Yet, in spite of this she has always continued to spread her message of truth, love, and salvation throughout the world while those who vowed to destroy Her have ended up in the dustbin of history. As Chesterton said, "on five occasions in history the Church has gone to the dogs, but on each occasion, it was the dogs that died."[16] Expressive Individualists today are also bent on silencing Christianity, but we have the sure supernatural hope that the Church will prevail. As Saint Pope John-Paul II told us:

> There is no evil to be faced that Christ does not face with us. There is no enemy that Christ has not already conquered. There is no cross to bear that Christ has not already borne for us, and does not now bear with us. And on the far side of every cross we find the newness of life in the Holy Spirit, that new life which will reach its fulfillment in the resurrection. This is our faith. This is our witness before the world.[17]

16   Gilbert Chesterton, *The Everlasting Man*, June 24, 2021, Part 2, Chapter 6, https://www.gutenberg.org/files/65688/65688-h/65688-h.htm.

17   John Paul II, "Homily of his Holiness, John Paul II, at Oriole Park in Camden Yards, Baltimore," October 8, 1995, sec. 5, https://www.vatican.va/content/john-paul-ii/en/homilies/1995/documents/hf_jp-ii_hom_19951008_baltimore.html.

> Do not be afraid... So often today man does not know what is within
> him, in the depths of his mind and heart. So often he is uncertain
> about the meaning of his life on this earth. He is assailed by doubt, a
> doubt which turns into despair. We ask you therefore, we beg you with
> humility and trust, let Christ speak to man. He alone has words of life,
> yes, of eternal life.[18]

A final reason for our hope is that we are living in a time of crisis, and times of crisis are good times for the Church. With all that is going on, many of the old certainties are being called into question. People are realizing that the sexual revolution, radical feminism, and rampant consumerism have not brought fulfillment and happiness. People are looking for new ideas and new solutions. And that creates an opportunity for Christians. Even though the First Christians had no power and were persecuted, their faith and virtuous conduct transformed the world. This will happen again.

How is the Christian going to go about influencing the culture? He should first of all remember that he is perfectly entitled to take his rightful place as a citizen in the heart of civil society. That is where he belongs. He is not *like* the others. That expression already implies a difference. They are his peers, his equals. The street is his rightful place. He must reject the notion that he is somehow infiltrating society. And he has as much right as anyone to express his ideas about the best way to order society and to shape the culture. And his proposals deserve as much of a hearing in the market place of ideas as those of anyone else.

If he is going to be salt, light, and leaven in the heart of civil society, the Christian layperson must not be perceived by those in his milieu as a foreign element. He should not be seen as someone weird who has come in from another planet. Because in fact he has not. He belongs there—in the university, in the law firm, in the pub, in a family gathering—as much as anyone. And he has every right to bear witness to his faith when he is with his colleagues, friends, neighbours, and relatives. But how will he do this? Of course, if he wishes, he can make a bold public statement about who he is. He can wear a large cross around his neck or sport a shirt that says "10 good reasons to be Christian," or evangelize by going door to door or preaching in the park. By giving a public, external witness of this sort to his Faith, he is undoubtedly showing courage. After all, he risks ridicule and will be marginalized by his peers. And yet, even though it takes courage to give this public witness, the bottom line is that the Christian who does this is unwittingly escaping from the more difficult task of having a far more effective though less spectacular effect on people. He may

---

18   John Paul II, "Homily of his Holiness John Paul II for the Inauguration of his Pontificate," October 22, 1978, sec. 5.

succeed in engaging some people in dialogue about the Faith, but never as one more among his colleagues.

In his book, *Search and Rescue*, Christian apologist Patrick Madrid gives a good example of the effectiveness of naturalness. He says that he does a great deal of traveling, and this often gives him the opportunity to engage in apostolic conversations with the person sitting beside him. When he is asked his profession by his fellow passenger, he says that he is a writer. And when he is asked what he writes about the subject of the Faith, it quickly comes up. This often leads to interesting and fruitful conversations. On the other hand, when he is tired and does not wish to engage in conversation, he follows a different plan. When asked what he does, he reaches slowly into his briefcase, pulls out his Bible, leans towards his neighbour with an intense gaze, and says with a smile, "I'm glad you asked. I'm a Christian Evangelist." This almost always has the effect of ending the conversation.[19]

Public witness is proper to priests and members of religious orders who are called by God to seek holiness in that way. One might say that they are called to imitate the public life of Christ. However, this is not the way of the layperson, who is called to imitate Christ's Hidden Life. We recall that when Christ began his public life, the people of Nazareth were astounded. He had lived among them for 30 years with such naturalness that they had never suspected that he was the Messiah. He was undoubtedly an exemplary and virtuous figure in Nazareth, but since his time had not yet come, he never did anything out of the ordinary. The same may be said of the Blessed Virgin Mary and St. Joseph. They were the two greatest saints in the history of the Church, and yet they attained great holiness by fulfilling their daily duties with love of God without any show or fanfare.

The lay person will live his Faith in his daily life with naturalness, without external signs. It is preferable that his colleagues come to know the Christian over time and be impressed with his professional competence and the way he lives the virtues in daily life. As they come to know him, they will learn that he is a practicing Christian who takes his faith seriously. People should encounter Christ in us and through us. Our aim should never be to intimidate anyone into an encounter with Christ, since by its very nature intimidation is incompatible with that encounter.

There is a deeply rooted prejudice to the effect that people who take their faith seriously do so as a sort of escape because they cannot succeed in the real world. A successful professional who also takes his faith seriously is seen as a rare exception. Christians have to overcome that prejudice, not by externals (since this will only reinforce the prejudice that men of faith are strange), but by living their faith with naturalness. Since he belongs in the heart of society, since

19   Patrick Madrid, *Search and Rescue*, 176.

it is his home, his milieu, he will naturally have an operative concern to build up the earthly city from within, passionately loving the world the way he loves his family. Of course he will bring a Christian perspective to all his endeavors, seeking to contribute to the Christian transformation of his society. However, he will also strive to make a contribution to human progress, which is a way of living charity and serving his fellow men. A Christian who is not concerned about human progress and concerns himself only with the hereafter is a poor example of what the modern lay Christian should be.

How will the Christian's faith stand out then? He will be the friendliest person, always joyful, serene, optimistic, with good humor, and in a good mood. He will be the one who is most sensitive to the needs of others, with a great spirit of service, generous, patient, and understanding with everyone. He will be one who works hard and well, is temperate and sober in his conduct, one who is a faithful father and husband, deeply in love with and dedicated to his family, who lives a refined respect towards members of the opposite sex. He will be loyal to his employer, to his friends, and to everyone, never speaking badly about anyone who is not present. He is someone who is not vain and does not boast. He will be known as a man of character, one who is principled, standing up for what he believes in without being belligerent, abrasive, or aggressive, but without compromising. And it is precisely the good example that the Christian gives in living these virtues that will lead others to be attracted to the Faith. Among his colleagues, neighbours, acquaintances, there will always be some who are drawn to his example and with whom he can strike up a solid friendship.

Friendship is key to having a positive, Christian influence on others and on the culture. And unfortunately, friendship as a value risks being lost in our society. A friend is someone with whom we feel comfortable. We trust him enough that we feel that we can open our heart to him without fear of betrayal. It implies sacrifice. A true friend is one who will always be there when his friend is in need. As the joke goes, "a friend will help you move, but a close friend will help you move a body!" Nevertheless, making friends in North America is not easy. Many people have a defensive barrier up and protect themselves against anyone outside their family becoming too close. They do not want to become vulnerable and risk being hurt. And they are not ready to make the sacrifices that friendship calls for. For example, a recent survey showed that, although the average 18 to 35 year-old has 237 Facebook friends, when asked how many they could rely on in a crisis, the average answer was two. A quarter said one. An eighth said none.[20]

---

20   Gillan Scott, "Why it matters that Christianity has become alien to a lost generation of young people," *God and Politics in the U.K.,* June 26, 2013, https://godandpoliticsuk. org/2013/06/26/why-it-matters-that-christianity-has-become-alien-to-a-lost-generation-of-young-people/; Robin Dunbar, "Do online social media cut through the constraints that limit the size of offline social networks?" *Royal Society Open Science* 3, no. 1, January 1, 2016, https:// royalsocietypublishing.org/doi/10.1098/rsos.150292.

We need to connect with people and break down the barriers they have erected. We need to be people who are open, warm, friendly, and affectionate, ready to speak about ourselves and our family. Bolstered by our daily prayer and sacrifice for others, it is possible to win people over with love. Cheerfulness, optimism, and good humour are an important part of the Christian witness that attracts people to Christianity. And this cheerfulness should be part of the spiritual DNA of every Christian. For if I know myself to be a son of God, infinitely loved by my Father God, who is constantly watching out for me with his Divine Providence, how can I possibly be sad?

As Pope Francis has said,

> an evangelizer must never look like someone who has just come back from a funeral! Let us recover and deepen our enthusiasm, that "delightful and comforting joy" of evangelizing, even when it is in tears that we must sow… And may the world of our time, which is searching, sometimes with anguish, sometimes with hope, be enabled to receive the good news not from evangelizers who are dejected, discouraged, impatient or anxious, but from ministers of the Gospel whose lives glow with the fervour and joy of Christ.[21]

Msgr. Fernando Ocariz explains the importance of honest and respectful friendship as an outward sign of one's faith:

> In a real friendship, there is love and affection, and each one seeks the true good of the other person. It is a stable, firm and faithful relationship and matures as the friends spend time together. In a Christian, charity raises the love of friendship to the supernatural level, and so he seeks to love his friends with the love of Christ. This involves putting one's heart into his relationship with others, making a great effort to live empathy and to understand the convictions of his friends, even though he may never come to share them. He will stand firm on his own principles, without ever being aggressive, strident, abrasive or uncharitable.[22]

For the lay Christian, helping his family, friends, colleagues, neighbors, and relatives spiritually is part and parcel of his daily activity and not something distinct from his work, family life, and social life. He does not decide that at one point it is time to do some apostolate with someone. Rather than being someone

---

21 Francis, *Evangelii Gaudium*, encyclical letter, Vatican website, November 24, 2013, https://www.vatican.va/content/francesco/en/apost_exhortations/documents/papa-francesco_esortazione-ap_20131124_evangelii-gaudium.html#II.%E2%80%82The_delightful_and_comforting_joy_of_evangelizing, sec. 10.

22 Msgr. Fernando Ocariz, "Letter from the Prelate (1 November 2019)," Opus Dei, November 1, 2019, https://opusdei.org/en-ca/article/letter-from-the-prelate-1-november-2019/.

who does apostolate from time to time, he is quite simply an apostle all the time. In whatever he is doing, he is constantly giving an example of a virtuous life, and his conversation should always reflect his Christian worldview. This does not mean that he will lack naturalness, always turning the conversation to a religious subject or be preaching or lecturing to others. But his conversations will never be superficial. He will seek to raise the level of his discussions with others. If he prays about professional, political, economic, and social issues and brings his knowledge of Church teaching to bear on them, he will be able to offer others a more profound reflection on these issues. If they see that he has a well-thought-out approach to these questions and has resolved them in his own mind, they will be more likely to trust him and confide in him. And generally, his conversation will always be imbued with optimism, charity, loyalty, and the other virtues.

The Christian should fit right into his milieu; but he does not partake in conduct he considers inappropriate. He is in the world, but he is not worldly. "Do not be conformed to this world, but be transformed by the renewal of your mind."[23] There are times when he will simply have to be counter cultural. If his colleagues go out to a pub on Friday night after work he can join them, but he leaves after he has had a beer or two. We have testimonies from the first centuries showing that the Early Christians lived in the heart of society but did not attend the games in the forum or take part in the orgies or other forms of immoral behaviour. All of this is not secrecy. By acting in this way, the Christian is not hiding anything. He is simply living out his Christian vocation with naturalness.

And of course, he will be always seeking to influence his milieu for the good—to restore all things in Christ. And the way he goes about this will be determined by his own formation. That formation will be received from the Church. But the specific solutions he envisions to help create this kind of society will be his own. And he will often arrive at these solutions by applying the insights provided by his Faith to his particular area of work. The Christian will, however, never fall into the trap of thinking that his proposals constitute the official Christian position or that he is somehow representing the Church when he makes them. The Church has no official position on temporal issues such as politics, economics, social questions, etc. Her social doctrine sets out broad principles, but it is up to each layperson to find the best way of implementing those principles in the precise circumstances of each time and place. And different Christians may legitimately propose different solutions to a given social or political problem, and all these solutions may well be in conformity with the principles enunciated by the Church's teaching.

---

23   Romans 12:2 (Revised Standard Version: Second Catholic Edition).

The Christian will always respect the freedom of others. As we mentioned above, the Church has no dogmas on temporal issues. It has no official position on social, economic, or political questions. There is no Christian solution to free trade, campaign finance reform, or term limits. The Christian will avoid sectarianism and respect those who hold different opinions while continuing to defend his own. If he thinks someone is wrong, he always acts with great charity towards that person. Just as it would be wrong for the Christian to announce where he stands on the day he meets someone, it would be equally wrong if his colleagues did not come to know about his Faith little by little over a period of time.

> It is true that you have to live among the people of your time, in accordance with their mentality and customs, but always ready to give a reason for your hope in Jesus Christ. It should never happen that, simply because we have no need to adapt ourselves, being always among our peers, that we cannot be distinguished as disciples of Christ. How much sentimentalism, fear and cowardice there is in certain desires to adapt oneself to one's environment.[24]

Hence, we are called to "embrace the counter-cultural life of a committed Catholic in a secular age without resentment, regret or reluctance."[25] The Christian never hides his Faith. Although he never uses the excuse of his Faith to avoid legitimate professional obligations there are times when it will simply come out. If the group wants to meet on Sunday morning, he may have to say that he goes to Mass on Sunday morning. If he tries to hide his Faith, he will end up leading a double life. Anyone who comes to know him well has to learn that he is a man of Faith. So, the Christian has to ask himself, what is my goal? Is my goal a comfortable life, being the nice guy, well-liked by all? Or do I want to be true to my faith? If we live our faith, we will not be well liked by all, as Josemaria Escriva states:

> When the defense of truth is at stake, how can one desire neither to displease God nor to clash with one's surroundings? These two things are opposed: it is either one or the other! The sacrifice has to be a holocaust where everything is burned up, even the thought: "what will they say?" even what we call our reputation.[26]

If the Christian is struggling for holiness, trying to set a good example, or speaking with his colleagues or classmates, his conduct may be a moral slap

---

24 Josemaria Escriva, *Unpublished Letter* n.p., January 9, 1959, 25.

25 Colleen Campbell, *The Heart of Perfection* (Brentwood: Howard Books, 2019), 186.

26 Josemaria Escriva, *Furrow*, n.d., no. 34, https://escriva.org/en/surco/.

in the face to some, and they may react with hostility. In these situations, the Christian is called to overcome vanity and human respects and persevere in spite of opposition. He learns how to face inappropriate remarks, conversations, and situations with a supernatural naturalness. He will be so convinced of his way with such self-confidence, based not on any merits of his own but on his Faith in God, that he can handle these things dispassionately without doing anything strange.

It is no doubt true that, when faced with a woke, social justice warrior, he may not be able to make much headway. He will be accused of uttering hate speech and shouted down. In these situations, there is often no point in trying to make oneself heard, and direct confrontation is usually counter-productive. But after the fact, it will often be possible to approach those more moderate people who witnessed the exchange one by one and explore the issue with them. The Christian should never consider anyone his enemy. We are called to love everyone as Christ loved us. And who did Christ love? He loved everyone, even those who were torturing him to death. And how did he love us? To the last drop of his blood.

There is never reason to be rude, confrontational, or belligerent with anyone. As Cardinal Thomas Collins of Toronto has said, we should always engage others "with charity and clarity." If dialogue is not possible, the best course of action is to back off and pray for the person in question. We should be ready to suffer for our faith, but we have no obligation to seek out martyrdom. There is no need to grandstand. And the Christian should never adopt a negative, bitter zeal, lamenting the good old days and deploring the current situation. That is not appealing and is no way to win people to one's cause. Nor should he be always moralizing, talking down to people, and giving lessons. Escriva states that,

> The task for a Christian is to drown evil in an abundance of good. It is not a question of negative campaigns, or of being anti anything. On the contrary, we should live positively, full of optimism, with youthfulness, joy and peace. We should be understanding with everybody, with the followers of Christ and with those who abandon him, or do not know him at all. But understanding does not mean holding back, or remaining indifferent, but being active.[27]

The Christian should be joyful, optimistic, positive, and upbeat, a sower of peace and joy. Instead of giving lessons, he should be anxious to share with others the treasure he has discovered in his Faith. He should see his mission to evangelize the culture as high adventure, not a burden. C.S. Lewis has compared

---

27   Josemaria Escriva, *The Forge*, n.d., no. 864, https://escriva.org/en/forja/.

the world to enemy-occupied territory: "Christianity is the story of how the rightful king has landed, you might say landed in disguise, and is calling us to take part in a great campaign."[28]

I grew up in Montreal where drivers often have little respect for the rights of pedestrians. In fact, a bumper sticker that one sometimes sees reads, "So many pedestrians, so little time." The motto of the modern apostle can be similar: "so many souls, so little time." Indeed, "so many souls." In light of that consideration, we may be tempted to think that since I can only reach a very few of those souls myself, what is the point of even trying to evangelize the culture? I will have only a negligible effect. And furthermore, most of the souls whom I know are far from the faith and seem resistant to my efforts to help them.

When tempted to think like this, we should remember what Pope Benedict XVI tells us in Spe Salvi:

> It is never too late to touch the heart of another, nor is it ever in vain.[29] And we should also recall that wise and holy observation of St. Mother Teresa of Calcutta: God does not demand that I be successful. God demands that I be faithful. When facing God, results are not important. Faithfulness is what is important.[30]

We should seek to have a positive effect on everyone whom we meet, regardless of their attitude towards us. No soul should leave us indifferent.

And once again, we should look to the example of Our Lord. He doesn't reject anyone, no matter how wretched. When we read the Gospels we

> discover a good shepherd, who knows every sheep by name. We find a shepherd for whom every single individual sheep is so important that he would leave ninety-nine sheep in the wilderness to seek out one that strayed. We don't meet a Messiah of numbers or of percentages but a Messiah for whom every one counts. All it took was one person in need to move his heart. All it took was a single individual (even an unworthy, sinful individual) to set him in action. For Jesus, people were never numbers; they were always persons.[31]

---

28 Clive Lewis, *Mere Christianity* (New York: Harper Collins, 2001), 45-46.

29 Benedict XVI, *Spe Salvi*, Encyclical letter, Vatican website, November 30, 2007, sec. 48, https://www.vatican.va/content/benedict-xvi/en/encyclicals/documents/hf_ben-xvi_enc_20071130_spe-salvi.html.

30 Tom Perna, "Teresa of Calcutta: 12 Quotes on Faith and Holiness", Tom Perna, September 3, 2016, https://tomperna.org/2016/09/03/mother-teresa-12-quotes-on-faith-and-holiness/#:~:text=%E2%80%9CGod%20does%20not%20demand%20that%20I%20be%20successful.,are%20not%20important.%20Faithfulness%20is%20what%20is%20important.%E2%80%9D.

31 Thomas Williams, *A Heart Like His: Meditations on the Sacred Heart of Jesus* (New York: Circle Press, 2010), 52-54

He saw each one as being made in the image and likeness of God and each one was infinitely loved by him. For Our Lord, each person was unique and irreplaceable.

> He didn't distinguish between important people and unimportant people. All were of infinite worth to him. That's why Jesus makes time for everyone. That's why he treats each person with the same respect, no matter how wretched. Jesus never made "quality of life" judgments to see who deserved his attention and his care.[32]

For Jesus, every human life had infinite worth and value.

> Day after day, Christ devoted himself to real people, with names, addresses, personal histories, and individual needs. The Gospels … narrate his encounters with real-life people: widows, soldiers, prostitutes, paralytics, lepers, beggars, and so on. They tell us of Jesus' meeting with Jairus the synagogue official and Zacchaeus the tax collector and Simon the leper and of course, Mary Magdalene "from whom seven demons had gone out" (Lk 8:2). [33]

We read about his interaction with the woman caught in adultery, the Samaritan woman at the well and Bartimaeus, the blind beggar.

He speaks to them from a boat while they are seated on the shore. Or on the mountain. Or during a banquet. Or walking through the wheat fields. Or in their own home. And he approaches each one with naturalness, using language that they can understand. He uses the example of boats and nets when speaking with fishermen. Sowing seed and the harvest when speaking to farmers. He uses the example of the lost coin for housewives. And with the Samaritan woman he speaks about drawing water from the well. He welcomes everyone. He accepts their invitations. And when they don't invite him, he invites himself as in the case of Zacchaeus.

And Christ does not limit himself to healing physical infirmities. He responds to more than their physical needs. He sees each person's most significant spiritual needs and attends to them.

> And we shouldn't romanticize what these people were like to deal with on a daily basis. Jesus didn't love them because they were such fine people that one couldn't help but love them. Most of the people Jesus dealt with were petty, short-sighted, and deeply flawed. Some were cheats. Others

---

32   Williams, *A Heart Like His*, 52-54.
33   Williams, *A Heart Like His*, 52-54.

were scheming. Still others were lazy, lustful, and dishonest. Yet Jesus loved those people, the imperfect and often unpleasant ones.[34]

This should be an example for us. Our Lord sends us to evangelize the people he places in our path, one soul at a time, regardless of whether they seem likely to be open to our message or not.

It is true that we will be able to reach only a very small number of people compared to the many who do not know Christ. Yet, in the eyes of God, that is totally irrelevant. After all, Our Lord tells us that "there will be more joy in heaven over one sinner who repents than over ninety-nine righteous persons who need no repentance."[35]

Let's imagine for a moment the scene of the multiplication of the loaves and fish. Christ has just asked his twelve apostles to feed the thousands of men and women who have been listening to his preaching. Looking around, they are totally disconcerted, since his request seems impossible to fulfill. They only manage to gather a few loaves and fish, and yet that was sufficient for Our Lord to work the miracle and satisfy the hunger of those thousands of people.

Our Lord is asking us to provide spiritual nourishment to the souls we encounter. Like the Apostles, we may be disconcerted by the seeming impossibility of the task. But all Our Lord wants from us are our own paltry loaves and fishes: our talents and abilities and our resolve to place them at his service. That is all he has chosen to need in order to work miracles in souls through us. So let us embark on this great adventure with peace, joy, optimism, and eagerness, trusting not in our own efforts or talents but in the grace of God, confident that he will continue to draw souls to himself, as he has always done, "for all things are possible with God."[36]

---

34 Williams, *A Heart Like His*, 52-54.
35 Lk. 15:7 (Revised Standard Version: Second Catholic Edition).
36 Mk. 10:27 (Revised Standard Version: Second Catholic Edition).

Bibliography

Aikman, David. *Jesus in Beijing: How Christianity Is Transforming China and Changing the Global Balance of Power*. Washington, DC., Regnery, 2003.

Bellah, Robert N. et al. *Habits of the Heart: Individualism and Commitment in American Life*. Berkely University of California Press, 1996.

Berman, Harold J. *Law and Revolution*. Cambridge, MA, Harvard University Pres, 1985

Bihlmeyer, Karl. *Church History, Vol. 1, Christian Antiquity*. Westminster, MD, The Newman Press, 1968.

Bloom, Allan. *The Closing of the American Mind: How Higher Education Has Failed Democracy and Impoverished the Souls of Today's Students*. New York, NY Simon & Schuster Paperbacks, 1987.

Bonagura, David G. *Steadfast in Faith: Catholicism and the Challenges of Secularism*. Providence, RI, Cluny Media, 2019.

Bonnassie, Pierre. *From Slavery to Feudalism in South-Western Europe*. Cambridge, ENG, Cambridge University Press, 1991.

Budziszewski, J. *Natural Law For Lawyers*. USA, ACW Press and The Blackstone Legal Fellowship, 2006.

Budziszewski. J. *What We Can't Not Know: A Guide*. Dallas, TX, Spence, Publishing Company, 2003.

Burke, Cormac. *Man and Values - A Personalist Anthropology*. Strongsville, OH, Scepter Publishers, 2008.

Campbell, Colleen. *The Heart of Perfection*. Brentwood, NH, Howard Books, 2019.

Canadian Conference of Catholic Bishops. *Catechism of the Catholic Church Second Edition*. Ottawa, ON, Libreria Editrice Vaticana, 1997.

Canadian Conference of Catholic Bishops. *Compendium of the Social Doctrine of the Church: Pontifical Council for Justice and Peace*. Ottawa, ON, CCCB Publications, 2005

Charles SJ, Rodger. *An Introduction to Catholic Social Teaching*. Oxford, UK, Family Publications, 1999.

Chaput, Charles J. *Strangers in a Strange Land: Living the Catholic Faith in a Post-Christian World*. New York, NY, Henry Holt and Company, 2017.

Chesterton, G.K. *Twelve Modern Apostles and Their Creeds*. New York, Duffield & Company, 1926.

Chesterton, G.K. *What's Wrong with the World*. New York, Dodd, Mead and Company, 1910.

DeMarco, Donald. *Ten Major Moral Mistakes and How they are Destroying Society.* Corpus Christi, TX, Goodbooks Media, 2015.

Deneen, Patrick J. *Why Liberalism Failed.* VA, Yale University Press, 2018.

Dreher, Rod. *Live Not By Lies: A Manual For Christian Dissidents.* New York, NY, Sentinel, 2020.

Eberstadt, Mary. *It's Dangerous to Believe: Religious Freedom and It's Enemies.* New York, NY, HarperCollins books, 2016/

Eberstadt, Mary. *How the West Really Lost God.* West Conshohocken, PA, Templeton Press, 2013.

Eberstadt, Mary. *Primal Screams: How The Sexual Revolution Created Identity Politics.* West Conshohocken, PA, Templeton Press, 2019.

Esolen, Anthony. *Sex and the Unreal City: The Demolition of the Western Mind.* San Francisco, CA, Ignatius Press, 2020.

Ferngren, Gary B. *Medicine and Health Care in Early Christianity.* Baltimore, MD, John Hopkins University Press, 2009.

Feser, Edward. *The Last Superstition: A Refutation of the New Atheism.* South Bend, IN, St. Augustine's Press, 2008.

Garnsey, Peter. *Religious Toleration in Classical Antiquity.* Cambridge, ENG, Cambridge University Press, 2016.

Gay, Craig M. *The Way of the (Modern) World Or, Why It's Tempting to Live As If God Doesn't Exist.* Grand Rapids, MI, William B. Eerdmans Publishing Company, 1998.

Gimpel, Jean. *The Medieval Machine: The Industrial Revolution of the Middle Ages.* New York, Henry Holt & Company, Inc, 1976.

Goldberg, Jonah. *Suicide of the West: How the Rebirth of Tribalism, Populism, Nationalism, and Identity Politics is Destroying American Democracy.* New York, Crown Forum, 2018.

Goldberg, Jonah. *Liberal Fascism: The Secret History of the American Left from Mussolini to the Politics of Meaning* New York, Doubleday, 2008.

Gregg, Samuel. *Reason, Faith, and the Struggle for Western Civilization.* Washington D.C., Regnery Gateway, 2019.

Gregory, Brad, *The Unintended Reformation: How a Religious Revolution Secularized Society* Cambridge, MA, Harvard University Press, 2012.

Hanson, John Henry. *Home Again: A Prayerful Rediscovery of Your Catholic Faith.* New York, Scepter Publishers, 2020.

Havel, Vaclav. *The Power of the Powerless.* Armonk, NY, M. E. Sharpe, 1985.

Hill, John. *After the Natural Law.* San Francisco, CA, Ignatius Press, 2016.

Hogan, J. Michael. *Rhetoric and Reform in the Progressive Era.* East Lansing, MI, Michigan State University Press, 2003.

Holland, Tom. *Dominion: The Making of the Western Mind.* London, ENG, Little, Brown, 2019/

Kalb, James. *The Tyranny of Liberalism: Understanding and Overcoming*

Administered Freedom, Inquisitorial Tolerance, and Equality by Command. Wilmington, DE, ISI Books, 2008.

Kreeft, Peter. *Making Choices.* Cincinnati, OH, Servant Books, 1990.

Kreeft, Peter. *The God Who Loves You: "Love Divine, All Loves Excelling".* San Francisco, CA, Ignatius Press, 2004.

Lewis, Clive. *Mere Christianity.* New York, Harper Collins, 2001.

Macedo, Stephen. *Liberal Virtues.* Oxford, ENG, Clarendon Pres, 1990.

MacLeod, Adam J. *The Age of Selfies: Reasoning About Rights When the Stakes Are Personal.* London, ENG, Rowman & Littlefield, 2020.

Madrid, Patrick. *Search and Rescue: How to Bring Your Family and Friends into- or Back to- the Catholic Church.* Manchester, NH, Sophia Institute Press, 2012.

Manchester, William. *The Glory and the Dream, A Narrative History of America, 1932-1972.* Boston, MA, Little Brown, 1973.

Martin, Francis. *The Feminist Question.* Grand Rapids, MI, Eerdmans, 1994.

Mill, John Stuart, *On Liberty.* London, ENG, John W. Parker And Son, 1859.

Miller, Leila. *Primal Loss: The Now-Adult Children of Divorce Speak.*, LCB Publishing, 2017.

Needham, Joseph. *Science and Civilization in China Vol. 1.* Cambridge, ENG, Cambridge University Press, 1954.

Numbers, Ronald L., ed. *Galileo Goes to Jail: And Other Myths about Science and Religion.* Cambridge, MA, Harvard University Press, 2009.

Ocariz, Fernando Cf., Seco, L.F. Mateo and Riestra, J.A., *The Mystery of Jesus Christ.* Portland, OR, Four Courts Press, 1994.

Panzer, Joel. *The Popes and Slavery.* New York, Alba House, 1996.

Pernoud, Regine. *Women in the Days of the Cathedrals.* San Francisco, CA, Ignatius Press, 1988.

Petigny, Alan. *The Permissive Society in America, 1941-1965.* Cambridge, ENG, Cambridge University Press, 2009.

Phillips, Melanie. *The World Turned Upside Down: The Global Battle over God, Truth, and Power.* New York, NY, Encounter Books, 2010.

Rectenwald, Michael. *Beyond Woke.* London, ENG, New English Review Press, 2020.

Reilly, Robert R. *America on Trial: A Defense of the Founding.* San Francisco, CA, Ignatius Press, 2020.

Reilly, Robert. *The Closing of the Muslim Mind.* Wilmington, MA, ISI Books, 2010.

Reno, R.R. *Resurrecting the Idea of a Christian Society.* Washington D.C., Regnery Faith, 2016.

Rice, Charles. *50 Questions on the Natural Law: What It Is & Why We Need It.* San Francisco, CA, Ignatius Press, 1995.

Roback Morse, Jennifer. *The Sexual State: How Elite Ideologies are Destroying*

Lives and Why the Church was Right All Along. Charlotte, NC, TAN Books, 2018.

Rummel, R.J. *"61,911,000 Victims: Utopianism Empowered" in Lethal Politics: Soviet Genocide and Mass Murder Since 1917*. NB, Transaction Publishers, 1990.

Sabine, George H. and Thorson, Thomas L. *A History of Political Theory, 4th Edition*. Dryden Press, 1973.

Safranek, John P. *The Myth of Liberalism*. Washington D.C., The Catholic University of America Press, 2015.

Sartre, Jean-Paul. *Existentialism is a Humanism*, trans. Carol Macomber. New Haven, CT, Yale University Press, 2007.

Schlueter, Nathan W., Wenzel, Nikolai G. *Selfish Libertarians and Socialist Conservatives?: The Foundations of the Libertarian-Conservative Debate*. Stanford, CA, Stanford University Press, 2017.

Shah, Timothy Samuel and Hertzke, Allen D, ed., *Christianity and Freedom, Volume I: Historical Perspectives*, Cambridge, Cambridge University Press, 2016).

Siedentop, Larry. *Inventing the Individual: The Origins of Western Liberalism*. U.K. Penguin Books, 2014.

Socias, Rev. James. *Introduction to Catholicism for Adults*. Woodridge, IL, Midwest Theological Forum, 2012.

Solzhenitsyn, Aleksandr. *The Gulag Archipelago 1918-1956*. trans. Thomas Whitney, New York, Harper & Row, 1974.

Spencer, Nick. *The Evolution of the West: How Christianity has Shaped Our Values*. London, ENG, SPCK, 2016.

Sri, Edward. *Men, Women and the Mystery of Love*. Cincinnati, OH, Franciscan Media, 2015.

Stark, Rodney. *How The West Won: The Neglected Story of the Triumph of Modernity*. Wilmington, DE, ISI Books, 2014.

Stark, Rodney. *The Rise of Christianity*. Princeton, NJ, Princeton University Press, 1996.

Stark, Rodney. *The Victory of Reason: How Christianity Led to Freedom, Capitalism, and Western Success*. New York, NY, Random House Inc. 2005.

Swafford, Andrew. *What Does the Church Say about Capitalism?* West Chester, PA, Ascension Press, 2018.

Taylor, Charles, *A Secular Age*. Cambridge, Belknap, 2007.

Tierney, Brian. *The Idea of Natural Rights*. Atlanta, GA, Scholars Press, 1997.

Trasancos, Stacy. *Fr. Jaki and the Stillbirths of Science*. Catholic Education, 2014.

Trese, Leo. *The Faith Explained*. Fort Wayne, IN, Scepter Publishers, inc, 1965.

Trueman, Carl R. *The Rise and Triumph of the Modern Self*. Weaton, IL, Crossway, 2020.

Trueman, Carl R. *Strange New World: How Thinkers and Activists Redefined*

Identity and Sparked the Sexual Revolution. Wheaton, IL, Crossway, 2022.

Ullman, Walter. *Medieval Political Thought.* City of Westminster, ENG, Penguin Books, 1965.

Wilken, Robert Louis. *Liberty in the Things of God: The Christian Origins of Religious Freedom.* New Haven CT, London, ENG, Yale University Press, 2019.

Wiker, Benjamin. *10 Books That Screwed Up the World: and 5 Others That Didn't Help.* Washington, D.C. Regnery Publishing, 2008.

Williams, Thomas D. *A Heart Like His: Meditations on the Sacred Heart of Jesus.* USA, Circle Press, 2010.

Zmirak, John. *Disorientation: The 13 "isms" That Will Send You to Intellectual "La-La Land".* West Chester, PA, Ascension Press, 2010.

About the Author

Anthony Schratz is a retired lawyer and educator who has spent the past 40 years implementing leadership programs for youth. He has acquired expertise in Church History and has spoken at Apologetics conferences and other similar venues.

Since 2007 he has been the director of Ernescliff College, a university residence and formation centre for young men on the campus of the University of Toronto in which the activities of doctrinal and spiritual formation are entrusted to the Opus Dei Prelature.

Other Titles by True Freedom Press

Ed. Scott D. G. Ventureyra, *COVID-19: A Dystopian Delusion: Examining Machinations of Governments, Health Organizations, the Globalist Elites, Big Pharma, Big Tech, and the Legacy Media* (Ottawa, Canada: True Freedom Press, 2022).

Ed. Scott D. G. Ventureyra *Making Sense of Nonsense: Navigating through the West's Current Quagmire* (Ottawa, Canada: True Freedom Press, 2022).

Satirical-Gage Series

These are purely satirical series and not to be taken seriously.

Scott D. G. Ventureyra, *The Safe Bet: The 2020 Presidential Election Case for Joe Biden: A Brilliant Campaign and Forty-Seven Year of Unparalleled Dedication to the American People* (Ottawa, Canada: True Freedom Press, 2020).

Scott D. G. Ventureyra, *Beacons of Hope: A Thorough Investigation into the Morality and Intelligence of Justin Trudeau and Chrystia Freeland* (Ottawa, Canada: True Freedom Press, 2022).

Scott D. G. Ventureyra, *The Safe Bet: The 2020 Presidential Election Case for Joe Biden: A Brilliant Campaign and Forty-Seven Year of Unparalleled Dedication to the American People: Second Edition* (Ottawa, Canada: True Freedom Press, 2024).

Scott D. G. Ventureyra, *The Safe Bet! Part Deux: The ~~2020~~ 2024 Presidential Case for ~~Joe Biden~~: A Brilliant Campaign and ~~Forty-Seven~~ Fifty-One Years of Unparalleled Dedication to the American People: Ultimate Patriot Edition* (Ottawa, Canada: True Freedom Press, 2024).

These titles and others can be directly purchased through Amazon or True Freedom Press at https://truefreedompress.co/shop-books/.

If you require editing, typesetting, cover design, or publishing services, visit True Freedom Press at truefreedompress.co.

Index

www.ingramcontent.com/pod-product-compliance
Lightning Source LLC
Chambersburg PA
CBHW060249050426
42448CB00009B/1600